Cultivating
High-Quality Teaching
Through Induction
and Mentoring

This book is dedicated to my daughter Kristin, a beginning teacher who is on that challenging journey from survival to success and high-quality teaching. May her teaching career be as rewarding and fulfilling as mine has been.

Carol A. Bartell

Cultivating
High-Quality Teaching
Through Induction
and Mentoring

Foreword by Linda Darling-Hammond

CORWIN PRESS
A Sage Publications Company
Thousand Oaks, California

For information:

Corwin Press
A Sage Publications Company
2455 Teller Road
Thousand Oaks, California 91320
www.corwinpress.com

Sage Publications Ltd
1 Oliver's Yard
55 City Road
London EC1Y 1SP
United Kingdom

Sage Publications India Pvt. Ltd.
B-42, Panchsheel Enclave
Post Box 4109
New Delhi 110 017 India

Printed in the United States of America

Library of Congress Cataloging-in-Publication Data

Bartell, Carol A.
Cultivating high-quality teaching through induction and mentoring / Carol A. Bartell.
    p. cm.
Includes bibliographical references and index.
ISBN 0-7619-3858-3 (cloth) — ISBN 0-7619-3859-1 (pbk.)
    1. Teachers—In-service training—United States. 2. Teacher orientation—United States.
3. Mentoring in education—United States. I. Title.
LB1731.B28 2005
370'.71'5—dc22

                                    2004014286

This book is printed on acid-free paper.

05   06   07   08   09   10   9   8   7   6   5   4   3   2   1

Acquisitions editor:	Rachel Livsey
Editorial assistant:	Phyllis Cappello
Production editor:	Sanford Robinson
Copy editor:	Richard H. Adin, Freelance Editorial Services
Typesetter:	C&M Digitals (P) Ltd.
Cover designer:	Tracy Miller
Indexer:	Molly Hall

Contents

About the Author   ix

Foreword   xi
Linda Darling-Hammond

Preface   xv

Acknowledgments   xix

1. **The Challenges Facing Beginning Teachers**   1
    A Case of Beginning Teaching   1
    The Challenges of Beginning Teaching   3
    The Need for Teachers   4
    Induction Defined   5
    Preparation to Teach   6
    Routes into Teaching   7
    New Teacher Motivations and Career Choice   9
    Teacher Collaboration   11
    The Teaching Context   12
    Other Challenging Contexts   13
    Teacher Motivations and Induction Planning   14
    A Planned Induction Period for All Beginning Teachers   15
    Meeting the Needs During a Planned Induction Period   16
    Implications for Practice   18

2. **Understanding the Stages of Teacher Development**   21
    From Preparation to Practice   21
    Continued Learning   22
    Teaching as a Profession   23
    Teacher Career Stages   24
    The Development of Teaching Expertise   26
    Stage Theories and Induction   29

Teacher Development in Context 30
The Induction Stage 32
Bridging Preparation and Practice 33
Psychological Stages for the First-Year Teacher 34
School Context and the Beginning Teacher 35
The Induction Stage and the Alternate-Route Teacher 37
Implications for Practice 41

3. The Characteristics of Effective Induction Programs **43**
Effective Induction Programs 43
The Organization of Effective Induction Programs 44
Program Purposes 45
Induction Program Leadership 47
Collaboration in Induction Services 48
Support of Site Administrators 49
University Linkages 50
Attention to Context 53
Experienced Teachers as Support Providers 58
Time to Work Together 59
Professional Development for New Teachers 61
Follow-up by Experienced Educators 64
Feedback to Beginning Teachers 65
Evaluation of the Program 65
Implications for Practice 66

4. Mentoring Strategies and Best Practices **71**
The Role of Mentoring in Induction 71
The Concept of Mentoring 72
The Benefits of Mentoring 73
Mentoring Toward a Vision 75
Selection of Mentors 75
Matching Mentors to New Teachers 79
Time for New Teachers and Mentors to Work Together 80
Mentor Compensation 81
Mentor Growth and Development 81
A Plan for the Mentoring Experience 83
Intensity of Mentoring Practices 83
Mentoring Challenges 86
Mentoring the Underprepared Teacher 87
Implications for Practice 90

5. Urban Schools and Induction **93**
Induction and the Urban Setting 93
Unsatisfactory Academic Achievement 94

Political Conflict		95
Inexperienced Teaching Staff		95
Turnover of Administrators		96
Low Expectations and Lack of Demanding Curriculum		97
Lack of Instructional Coherence		98
High Student Mobility		98
Poor Facilities and Unsafe Neighborhoods		98
Teacher-Student Mismatch		99
The Case for Teaching in Urban Settings		100
Induction in the Urban Setting		101
Teachers for Diverse Urban Schools		104
Toward Cultural Proficiency		106
Mentors for Urban Schools		107
Merged Preparation and Induction		109
Implications for Practice		111
6.	**Standards-Based Teaching and Reflective Practice**	**115**
	Induction Focus	115
	The Concept of Reflective Practice	116
	Standards for a Profession	118
	Standards-Based Induction	120
	National Standards for Beginning Teachers	121
	State Standards: California	123
	Standards-Based Practice	124
	Student Standards	127
	The INTASC Standards and Reflective Practice	128
	The CSTP and Reflective Practice	130
	Reflective Mentoring	131
	Reflective Practice in the Induction Years	132
	Some Cautions About Reflective Practice	134
	Reflection in Community	135
	Tools to Enhance Reflection	136
	Where Does Standards-Based Reflection Lead?	138
	Implications for Practice	139
7.	**Teacher Assessment**	**143**
	Standards-Driven Assessment	143
	Induction Assessments in Context	146
	Assessments in Induction	147
	Ongoing Evaluation of Teaching	147
	Formative and Summative Assessments	148
	Assessment Approaches	149
	Examples of Performance-Based Assessments in Practice	152

INTASC Assessments   153
The BTSA Assessment System   154
Locally Developed Assessments   159
Using Assessment to Advance Reflective Practice   160
Implications for Practice   161

8. Developing Induction Policies to Shape Induction Practices   165
A Vision of Teacher Induction   165
Teacher and Student Success   167
Local Induction Policies   168
State Policy   168
The Continuum of Development in California   170
The Federal Role   172
From Policy to Practice   173
The Future of Induction   175
Implications for Practice   175

References   **177**

Index   **183**

About the Author

 **Carol A. Bartell** has been interested in teacher induction since 1988, when she first became involved with what was then the California New Teacher Project, a pilot project with fifteen districts in California. Her role was first as a faculty member at the University of Pacific in Stockton, and shortly after as a staff member at the California Commission on Teacher Credentialing, and finally, as a member of the Commission representing the independent California Colleges and Universities in her role as Dean of the School of Education at California Lutheran University. Her interest in assisting teachers in urban schools led her to accept, beginning in the fall of 2003, the position of Dean of the Charter College of Education at California State University, Los Angeles.

Dr. Bartell has worked on a number of efforts related to teacher induction. She served as project officer for the evaluation of the California induction programs, led the initial state task force that developed the California Standards for the Teaching Profession, and led the development of the peer review process for the Beginning Teacher Support and Assessment Program. She has served on a number of national task forces and Commissions related to induction, including the National Commission on Professional Development and Support of Novice Teachers sponsored by the Association of Teacher Educators and Kappa Delta Pi, and the Interstate New Teacher Assessment and Support Consortium (INTASC).

Before Dr. Bartell entered the state policy and the higher education arena, she was a teacher. Her P-12 teaching career spans eleven years in five different states in urban, rural, and suburban settings. She remembers what it was like to begin anew as a novice in a different teaching context. She still enjoys getting into the classroom, when her schedule permits, to work with university students preparing for that very important work in schools.

Foreword

For many years, the metaphor most widely used to describe entry into teaching has been "sink or swim." The image this conjures—one of novice teachers bobbing up and down in a sea of raging waters, buffeted by high waves and clutching at a skimpy life preserver—is one that most educators are deeply familiar with. Most can recall in vivid and often painful detail the first rites of passage during their trial years in the class-room. Many former teachers in all walks of life will recount how they did not make it through. How they became discouraged when they were unable to translate into successful practice what they thought they had learned through their preparation programs or their "apprenticeship of observation" as students in schools themselves. They are in plentiful com-pany. About one third of people who enter the teaching profession leave within the first five years of teaching, and the ratios can be higher in schools with the greatest challenges and fewest supports.

Fortunately, this longstanding pattern has begun to change. Most states have launched some kind of mentoring or induction program for beginning teachers—though these vary widely in quality—and the notion that novice teachers should be supported in developing their practice, just as novice doctors, nurses, and engineers are, has become widely accepted, if not practiced.

Carol Bartell's timely and important book contributes to these efforts in a critically important way. Like many others, this book emphasizes the importance of the early years of teaching and the need for a careful, thoughtful plan for bringing newcomers into the profession. Going beyond these general calls for support, Bartell focuses on the need for a vision of good teaching to guide the mentoring and induction experience and describes how the substantive work of learning to teach can be guided and achieved.

Carol Bartell is uniquely qualified to write this book, having worked extensively with the leading efforts to develop standards for teacher licensing during the 1990s. She worked with the Interstate New Teacher

Assessment and Support Consortium—an organization of more than 30 states that crafted the first nationwide guidelines outlining knowledge, skills, and dispositions for beginning teacher licensing—and with the California Beginning Teacher Support and Assessment efforts that brought these standards to life through a massive mentoring and assessment initiative in the state of California. Both efforts have helped us better understand the importance of standards-based support during the crucial entry period into teaching. Both efforts have also recognized the need to assess teacher progress and to use the results of those assessments to nurture and support teacher development.

California has been involved in piloting, implementing, and studying the induction of new teachers since the late 1980s. It is one of very few states that have included an induction experience in the credentialing structure. Bartell summarizes that work in a way that is useful to those developing and implementing induction programs in California and elsewhere. She gives research-based, concrete examples of how successful programs can operate to support careful and thoughtful teacher development. She probes the motivations to teach, traces the development of teaching expertise, and the incentives to keep teachers learning and growing during the early years and beyond. Finally, she lays out a framework for local and state policies needed to support and sustain induction and mentoring programs.

The examples and teacher quotations included in the book ground the work in the lives and experiences of beginning teachers. Their words remind us of the challenges facing beginning teachers in contemporary classroom settings. They also highlight the importance of high-quality mentoring during the induction period.

If teachers are viewed primarily as transmitters of knowledge, one could argue that they need little more than basic content knowledge and the ability to impart this knowledge to students. But teachers are expected to do much more than pass along information. They must be prepared to serve as diagnosticians, planners, facilitators, and leaders who know a great deal about the learning process and have a wide repertoire of strategies at their disposal. They must understand their students as individual learners and take responsibility for engaging each and every student in authentic and powerful learning. It is the latter, more complex vision of teaching that guides this book.

This vision also requires that teachers are thoroughly grounded in subject matter and pedagogy during their preparation years, but are never considered to be "finished products." They continue to learn, develop, and perfect their teaching throughout their careers as they interact with students and their colleagues. Induction then becomes a bridge from a strong preservice preparation to expert practice that is honed and refined over time.

Teacher attrition continues to be an issue for all schools, and it particularly impacts urban settings, where salaries are lower, working conditions are more challenging, fewer well-prepared and experienced teachers remain, and students are frequently least well served. To solve the problems of high-turnover schools, districts need not only to hire highly qualified teachers but also to sustain and support them in their efforts to improve student learning. Bartell tackles the tough and crucial need to give special focus to the induction of new teachers in urban schools. She also deals with the knotty problem of serving the underprepared teacher who enters teaching through alternative routes, arguing for a thoughtful blending of a preparation and induction experience that does not shortchange the teacher or, most important, the students.

However, Bartell argues that induction is about more than retaining teachers. It is about helping all teachers become more professional and better at what they do. It is about using the expertise of experienced teachers to guide the novice teacher. It is about giving teachers careful and thoughtful feedback on their work. And, most importantly, it is about improving student learning.

Linda Darling-Hammond
Stanford University

Preface

The initial years of teaching are the most challenging for new teachers. Typically, new teachers are struggling to survive day-to-day. It is during these entry years that teachers are most likely to become disillusioned and leave their initial teaching positions or even the profession. For those who stay, the early years are ones in which teachers establish patterns and practices that often last throughout their career.

The realization of the importance of these early years has led us to give special attention to the induction phase of teaching—most frequently defined as the first one to three years. Teachers need to be guided and supported during these early years. We want teachers to be able to do more than just survive. We want them to become successful, contributing members of a profession.

One of the longest running and best-funded state-sponsored induction programs has been operating in California. The Beginning Teacher Support and Assessment (BTSA) program has grown from pilot project involving fifteen districts beginning in 1988 to a statewide effort and a permanent part of the credential structure. During that time, educators have learned a great deal from the extensive research on this program as well as other programs around the country. This book draws heavily, but not exclusively, on the research and experience with teacher induction in California in the last two decades. It includes the voices of new teachers, their mentors, and those who direct induction programs and activities. It also incorporates findings from some key national efforts.

Teacher induction takes on special meaning in the context of contemporary schools, where student achievement gaps have been put in the spotlight by recent accountability efforts. What are the special challenges of inducting teachers in urban schools where the turnover is high and many teachers are not fully certified? How do we help all teachers so that all students can be successful? What are the specific concerns and issues noted by teachers who enter with a full academic preparation? How can these new teachers be assisted so that they can be more effective in the classroom and contribute to enhanced learning for their students? How can all teachers be nurtured, supported, and developed so that they will be successful and will become contributing career professionals?

In this book, I focus on new teachers' needs and the strategies that are a part of an effective induction experience. I take into account the challenges of beginning teachers at varying points of readiness and in a variety of school contexts.

While much has been written about mentoring, less attention has been paid to the broader view of the entire induction experience. Induction and mentoring are too often narrowly focused on the "survival-level" strategies teachers need to cope with the demands of their first few years of teaching. While these initial survival strategies are important, the teacher development literature indicates that good teaching develops over time and that teachers have different learning needs at particular stages of their career. Teachers need to look beyond merely surviving and begin early to focus on student achievement and success in their own long-term professional development.

This book will help those who plan and implement induction programs to use strategies that foster new teacher and student success. Each chapter begins with a brief introduction to frame the major points discussed in the chapter. The chapter concludes with some implications for practice and suggested further readings.

Chapter 1 begins with a description of the challenges that new teachers face and defines the need for a strong induction program that is geared to the needs of individual new teachers. Chapter 2 looks at stages of teacher development, with an emphasis on teacher induction as a specific career stage that needs special attention. It also highlights the need to consider that induction occurs within a specific context. Chapter 3 outlines the key elements of an effective plan for induction and Chapter 4 discusses the role of effective mentoring in the induction program. Chapter 5 focuses on induction in the most challenging setting of urban schools. In Chapter 6, the point is made that induction programs should seek to move teachers beyond the survival stage and engage teachers in a critical look at their own practice and the learning of their students. Chapter 7 encourages induction planners to include an assessment of teaching in the induction period to foster reflective practice. Models and approaches are presented. The final chapter addresses induction policies and practices for local schools, districts, and states, and concludes with a vision for the future of induction.

The boxed quotations are drawn from interviews with teachers and their support providers in California, unless otherwise indicated. These quotations are included to bring the concepts to life and ground them in actual practice.

Throughout the book, there is an emphasis on the following:

- A developmental approach to assisting and supporting new teachers that moves teachers to a higher level of accomplished practice;

- A focus on induction in all settings, with special emphasis on the most challenging, hard-to-staff school settings; and
- A vision of teaching and learning that extends beyond the "survival level" and focuses on engaged student learning.

This book will help district and school administrators, mentors/support providers, staff developers, and others to develop and implement induction programs that focus on improved practice and high levels of accomplishment. It will help teacher educators understand and better prepare teachers for entry into the world of schooling. It will help policy makers understand how to shape induction policies that lead to teacher retention and improved student achievement.

Acknowledgments

I wish to acknowledge the many colleagues with whom I have worked who have helped shaped my own thinking and practice about teacher induction. Although they are too numerous to mention individually, they include the members of the Interagency Task Force from the California Commission on Teacher Credentialing and the California Department of Education, Directors of induction programs in the California New Teacher Project (1988–1992) and the Beginning Teacher Support and Assessment (BTSA) Program (1992 to present), members of the Task Force to develop the California Standards for the Teaching Profession, members of the National Commission on Professional Development and Support of Novice Teachers sponsored by the Association of Teacher Educators and Kappa Delta Pi, and members of the Interstate New Teacher Assessment and Support Consortium (INTASC). I certainly thank all of the new teachers and support providers who have shared their stories and perspectives with me. Finally, I thank California Lutheran University for providing me with a sabbatical so that I could take time away from my administrative responsibilities as dean and visit urban schools to talk with new teachers and update my own knowledge of the context for my work.

The contributions of the following reviewers are gratefully acknowledged:

Daryl M. Eason, Ed.D.
Adjunct Professor of Special Education
San Diego State University
San Diego, CA

Barbara L. Brock, Ed.D.
Associate Professor
Creighton University
Omaha, NE

Susan Villani, Ed.D.
Senior Program/Research Associate
Learning Innovations at WestEd
Stoneham, MA

Roberta Richin
Cofounder
Connecting Character to Conduct, Inc.
Stony Brook, NY

Margaret G. Olebe, Ph.D.
Director, Institute for Urban Literacy Research
California State University, Dominguez Hills
Carson, CA

1

The Challenges Facing
Beginning Teachers

New teachers bring varying backgrounds, motivations, experiences, and preparation levels to their initial teaching experience. Their view of the profession and their role in it is shaped by these motivations, as well as by the context in which they begin their work. This chapter explores the commitments that new teachers bring to their roles and the challenges they face. It sets forth the need for the development of a comprehensive induction program to help all new teachers become fully committed and more effective in the classroom.

A CASE OF BEGINNING TEACHING

Anna was a first-year teacher in an urban school. Although Business was her undergraduate major, she found her initial foray into the business world to be very unsatisfying. She wanted a career that would allow her to make a contribution to society. She heard about the need for teachers—particularly for math teachers—in her area. Not being quite sure what she needed to do to become eligible to work in a teaching capacity, she attended a recruitment fair put on by the local school district. There she heard about the program that would allow her to begin teaching while she completed work on a teaching credential through a district-led or a university-led alternative certification program.

After taking a test that measured her "basic skills" (reading, math, and writing), she was sent on some interviews at several middle schools. She was hired immediately and was told to sign up for a credential program. She was accepted into a program at a nearby university. She chose the university program because she knew she could earn a credential and a master's degree at the same time. However, she knew it would take two or more years, including summers, at a pretty intensive pace.

Because she was hired two weeks before school began, she began teaching before she was able to take any coursework. The district put her through a three-day orientation that covered the basics. However, she hardly felt that she was prepared for that first day.

She was assigned to teach five math sections, but they required four different preparations and she was required to move to three different classrooms during the day. There weren't enough books for all of her students and she didn't know when they would arrive. She knew about the state standards for students, because they were discussed in her orientation. However, she was perplexed because her students seemed to lack so many of the necessary underlying skills and prior knowledge that would allow them to work at the expected level. She scrambled to find material that was more appropriate to their skills.

Anna was assigned a mentor; he was an English teacher who was able to help her understand the expectations of teachers at her school. However, he did not know much about teaching math. Among her colleagues in the math department, the most senior had been teaching for just three years and was new to that particular school. He had just finished earning his credential. The four math teachers met together regularly, but they wished they had someone else who was a little more experienced to offer advice about the instructional program.

After several months, with the help of her mentor and the math team, Anna felt that she had established some fairly workable classroom management procedures. However, students were not making the progress in math that she had hoped. She assigned homework, but many students just did not turn it in. She called parents, but that did not seem to help. She had difficulty keeping up with all of the demands on her own time. It seemed like she spent many late hours grading papers, planning, and developing new resources.

Her classes at the university added to her stress. She was taking two classes back-to-back on Thursday nights. She was having difficulty keeping up with all the readings and assignments. Some of the readings and assignments seemed applicable to her own situation, but many of them did not.

Her mentor occasionally stopped in and asked if there was anything he could help her with. She didn't know how to respond to his vague offers of assistance. Although her district offered some new-teacher seminars, she just could not find the time to attend.

Anna survived a very demanding, stressful first year. However, she wasn't sure if she wanted to return the next year or if she wanted to continue to pursue teaching as a career.

THE CHALLENGES OF BEGINNING TEACHING

Beginning teachers enter classrooms today with high expectations for themselves and for their students. Yet, we know that the first year of teaching is a sobering experience for most new teachers, and that, over the course of one year, teachers experience a decreased strength of belief in their own efficacy and in the learning potential of their students (Harris and Associates, Inc., 1991). Nearly every study of retention in the teaching profession identifies the first three years as the riskiest on the job, the years in which teachers are most likely to leave. The drop out rate is highest among teachers in hard-to-staff, urban schools, which have the most difficulty both attracting and then retaining fully certified teachers (Ingersoll, 2001; Urban Teacher Collaborative, 2000).

The early years of teaching are often characterized by a "sink-or-swim" or "survival" mentality because we have often failed to provide for careful support and thoughtful development of teaching expertise over time. Beginning teachers are traditionally expected to assume all the same responsibilities as the more experienced teachers, and are often assigned the most difficult and challenging students, those that their more experienced colleagues do not want to teach. There is no staging or levels of responsibilities as there is in many other professions. It should not be a surprise that new teachers often speak of just trying to survive during their initial years in the classroom.

> My first year of teaching was way too stressful. I was not given a curriculum or materials to work with. There were too many kids and not enough desks or books. I really didn't know what I was expected to teach.
>
> Second-year teacher

Many support programs for new teachers focus on the teacher who enters the classroom having been through a comprehensive preparation program. Even the most well-prepared teachers need assistance in applying what they have learned and in moving from a student-teaching situation to their own classroom where they are now fully in charge. For the increasing numbers of teacher who enter classrooms without strong academic and professional preparation, the challenges are magnified.

> I was hired late, after school started. I missed the early orientation. Because I was the last one hired, I got students taken out of other classes. They really didn't want to leave their friends. I got the kids no one else wanted.
>
> First-year teacher

This book is written for those who want to change the way all new teachers are brought into the profession. It is focused on the induction of all new teachers, but gives special attention to induction in our most challenging settings—those where teachers and their students are least likely to experience success. It will help those who plan and implement induction programs to use strategies that help to retain new teachers and help them to become more successful in the classroom.

THE NEED FOR TEACHERS

The need for well-qualified, highly competent teachers has never been greater. Schools nationally will need to hire more than 2.2 million teachers to serve growing student enrollments and to replace the considerable number of teachers expected to retire (National Commission on Teaching and America's Future, 1996). All who prepare teachers are challenged to produce enough high-quality teachers to meet the demands. School districts are making enormous efforts to attract those who are fully prepared to teach or, in many cases, hiring those who may not be qualified but demonstrate the potential to develop teaching expertise. Yet, these preparation and recruitment efforts will not pay off if teachers are not retained or the new workforce does not help us meet the high standards we are setting for all of our students.

The extraordinary need for more teachers comes at a time in which the demands on teachers are increasing. Schools are expected to serve an increasingly diverse population and to provide more educational and other services to students and their families than ever before. These new teachers will teach in a wide variety of contexts and settings. They will teach in urban, rural, and suburban schools. They will teach the rich, the middle class, and the poor. They will teach students who are more ethnically, culturally, and linguistically diverse than any country in the world. They will teach students who have strong family support and a caring, nurturing environment, and many who lack this support system. They will teach students at a variety of ability levels and with a variety of learning needs.

At the very time it has become necessary to produce more teachers, we are called upon to prepare a more capable workforce—one that is well prepared for the challenges and complexities of the years ahead. State and national policy makers have embraced the "standards movement" calling for more accountability for teachers, students, and schools. These new teachers are expected to be "highly qualified" and will be held accountable for results in their classrooms (U.S. Department of Education, 2002).

> I know how important it is for my kids to do well on those tests. I keep the standards before them. I post them on the board and we talk about them. . . . I let them know what they are supposed to be learning with each lesson. I want them to do well.
>
> Third-year teacher

These challenges call for large numbers of new teachers who meet the minimum qualifications, pass all the required tests, and successfully complete increasingly demanding preparation programs. However, a sufficient workforce that meets minimum qualifications will not be enough to meet the challenges ahead. Teaching is difficult and challenging work. Teaching well so that all students develop their full potential and experience success is even more challenging.

Teachers coming into the profession today should expect that they will take the time to nurture and develop their knowledge, skills, and abilities to become expert at what they do. We hope that they care deeply about their work and their students, but they must be more than well intentioned. They should be able to critically examine, reflect upon, and perfect their own practice as they continually seek to acquire new knowledge and expertise.

For these reasons, we have ceased to think of learning to teach as limited to the time spent in an initial preparation program of a defined length. Learning to teach is a lifelong process, one that involves new learning as one comes in contact with each new student and shares ideas, problems, and solutions with colleagues. A crucial phase in this teacher development cycle is the induction, or entry period.

INDUCTION DEFINED

The initial years of service are generally considered to be the first one to three years of teaching. We have come to think of these years as the induction period, or the time in which the novice becomes more familiar with their job responsibilities, the work setting, and professional norms and expectations.

The entry period is a crucial time in the development of a teacher. Ideas, approaches, and practices learned during these early years will often be those that the teacher continues to rely upon throughout the teacher's career. We can leave teachers to struggle or get by as best they can during this period, or we can structure and guide this entry period so that it is a period of rich, continued learning and development that leads to success and expert practice.

Induction programs have been developed as a way to effectively and thoughtfully introduce new teachers to their responsibilities and bring newcomers into the profession. The goal of systematically planned program of induction is to help new teachers not just survive, but to succeed and thrive.

> *Teacher Induction Program: A systematic, organized plan for support and development of the new teacher in the initial one to three years of service.*

PREPARATION TO TEACH

Today's teachers come to the profession through an increasing range and types of preparation programs. Consequently, it is important for those who plan the induction experience to know what understandings and skills the new teacher brings to that initial teaching experience.

Many teachers, primarily those we call the "early deciders," take the traditional route to teaching, preparing to teach while they are in college, either in four- or five-year programs of study. They study the subject matter they will teach, earning the equivalent of a major or a minor in at least 38 states (National Association of State Directors of Teacher Education and Certification [NASDTEC], 2002). In addition to subject-matter knowledge and general liberal arts knowledge, the best of teacher preparation programs include the following in the knowledge base that is at the heart of learning and shaping professional practice:

- *Knowledge about learners and learning,* including knowledge about human growth and development, motivation and behavior, learning theory, learning differences, and cognitive psychology;
- *Knowledge about curriculum and teaching*, including general and content-specific pedagogical knowledge, curriculum theory, assessment and evaluation, and counseling, as well as knowledge of scientific inquiry, epistemology, communication, and language as they relate to pedagogy;
- *Knowledge about contexts and foundations of education,* including knowledge about schools and society, cultures, educational history and philosophy, principles from sociology and anthropology, legal responsibilities of teachers and ethics. (Darling-Hammond, Wise, & Klein, 1999, pp. 35–38)

To help new teachers begin to apply this knowledge to the classroom, most preparation programs include a range of guided field experiences under the tutelage of more experienced classroom teacher and/or a university supervisor.

Teacher's preservice programs differ in the approach they take to this learning and in the depth of knowledge and practice provided, but in general, teachers can be expected to bring this knowledge and experience to their first position. Nonetheless, these novices are hardly finished learning about the profession they have chosen to enter. Induction programs are intended not to reteach, but to build upon and extend that initial preparation experience.

However, increasingly numbers of teachers are entering the profession without even this basic preparation. Those who plan induction programs need to be aware of the level of preparation the new teacher brings.

ROUTES INTO TEACHING

While the more traditional approach to preparing teachers predominates, an increasing number of teachers come to teaching through what has been broadly termed "alternate routes." Because this term means different things in different state certification systems, the actual numbers entering though alternate routes are hard to measure. The alternatives range from completing an entire professional preparation program in an alternative format (evenings, weekends, summers) to programs that offer certification through demonstrated experience or assessment of knowledge and skills rather than formal training. Most often, alternate-route teachers begin to serve as teachers while they complete their coursework. Rather than undergoing the traditional student teaching experience under the guidance of an experienced teacher, they complete their directed teaching experience and demonstrate competence in their own classroom settings.

I graduated from a very prestigious university with a degree in civil engineering. However, after I graduated, I decided I didn't want to actually become an engineer. I went into it because I was good in math and it was sort of expected by my family. I did some volunteer work in urban schools along the way, and decided to give teaching a try—to see if I could be successful. I'm working on my credential while I teach. I plan to take next year off and go back and get a master's degree in urban education. I'm really committed to this now. I love working with the kids; they seem to respond well.

Second-year teacher

Some alternate-route teachers enter the classroom with little or none of the initial preparation described earlier. Although they may receive extensive on-the-job training by their own district or by a combination of university courses and staff development activities, they continue to learn while doing the important job of teaching.

Some individuals enter the profession immediately after they complete their preparation programs; others delay entry or do not enter at all. Others move across state lines and find that their preparation to teach in one state is considered incomplete in another. Some persons return to teaching after taking time out to raise a family or pursue other career options.

> I worked in the film industry. I'm a single dad. I was tired of the uncertainty of the job market and the crazy life with irregular hours. I always thought I would make a good teacher. I enjoy it immensely. It gives me a chance to use my creative talents with a very appreciative—for the most part—audience.
>
> Third-year teacher

All of these teachers have different learning needs depending on the background, preparation, and experience that they bring to the job. For example, an experienced teacher from Nebraska has much to offer when he moves to Michigan, but still needs to understand things such as the curriculum standards that guide programs in his new state of residence, and district and school policies that may differ from that of his last assignment. He may also be changing grade levels or moving from a rural to an urban setting. He needs to develop new relationships with colleagues and administrators and learn to fit into a new school and new community.

A teacher returning to the job market after several years spent raising a family faces a different set of needs. She brings increased experience with her own children and more life experience. But she will need to become knowledgeable about current curricular expectations and about the latest standards and assessment requirements for students.

The "downsized" computer programmer who decides to become a math teacher probably has a strong work ethic and experience in demanding environments that will stand her in good stead. She may have taught or trained other adults in the use of technology. She may possess knowledge of mathematic concepts, but may need to refresh her knowledge of content of the advanced math courses that she may not have been using in her work. Even if she taught adults, she will need help in relating to adolescents, and will probably need help in making that subject matter comprehensible to students, and in challenging and motivating them to be successful.

Successful plans for inducting new teachers will take into account these differences and recognize the need for differentiating services when supporting and mentoring new teachers for success with their students. An effective plan for support of all these new teachers will recognize and build on the knowledge and experience the beginning teacher brings to the classroom, assist teachers in gaining what is weak or lacking, and extend learning so that the teacher moves to higher levels of accomplished teaching.

NEW TEACHER MOTIVATIONS AND CAREER CHOICE

New teachers choose to enter teaching for a variety of reasons. Those motivations help explain why they chose to teach and how they will approach their work. It is helpful for those who will be working with new teachers to understand those motivations so they can help new teachers realize their goals for themselves and for their students.

Novice teachers today enter the profession with differing levels of preparation, experience, and expertise. Like the students they will serve, they come with a variety of expectations, hopes, dreams, and understandings. Some will go through a traditional teacher preparation program and will enter the job market immediately after graduation. Others will find their initial career choice unsatisfying and look for more satisfaction in teaching. Still others will seek a second career after early retirement from another, often very successful career,

---

I've always wanted to teach. My mother was a teacher and I came to school to volunteer in her classroom while I was in high school. I helped her with her bulletin boards and helped her get materials ready for her lessons. I'm teaching in the same school and the same classroom that she taught in for most of her career.

Second-year teacher

Most of these new teachers expect that they will be successful. Many are highly motivated and feel they will be able to positively influence student learning. Others are less certain about teaching as a career choice. However, all of these new teachers will help to shape the educational future of our nation. Together they will directly influence the learning of hundreds of millions of students over the course of their careers. Induction programs need to serve all of these new teachers.

It is worth examining the question of who selects teaching as a career and why they make that career choice. This knowledge makes it possible to intentionally begin to recruit those who demonstrate commitment and potential and then invest in their success. Teachers will be more inclined to stay and make a long-term contribution if they feel challenged and fulfilled in their work.

A study of 400 state and national Teachers of the Year (Goldberg and Proctor, 2000) indicates that the following are most important in the decision to enter teaching:

- Desire to work with children
- Love of subject matter
- Influence of a teacher
- Belief in the importance of teaching

Although this was a very selective group of teachers, their motivations are fairly typical of the highly successful teacher who remains vital and active in the profession. In general, teachers choose teaching over other options and see it as a positive and desirable choice. While some complain of the lack of monetary compensation and opportunity for advancement, these deterrents are usually overlooked because teachers seek other rewards and satisfactions.

Susan Moore Johnson and her colleagues have been studying what draws persons to the teaching profession for many years, examining the incentives to teach and what motivates and what matters to teachers. Her early work (Johnson, 1986) led to the conclusion that "better pay and higher status may draw those with an interest in teaching to the profession, but probably are not sufficient to retain or sustain outstanding staff members. Research indicates that the best teachers stay in teaching because of intrinsic rewards, although they may be forced to leave because of poor salary or working conditions" (p. 73).

This finding has been confirmed by her work and the work of others over the years. Johnson and her colleagues recently extended their research on teacher motivations in a project named "The Next Generation of Teachers." The recent research coming from this team at Harvard (Peske, Liu, Johnson, Kauffman, & Kardos, 2001) points out that the new generation differs from those that are about to retire in important ways. Their research suggests that, "rather than regarding teaching as a lifelong commitment, many new teachers—both those who completed traditional teacher preparation programs and those who did not—approach teaching tentatively or conditionally" (p. 305).

My long-term goal is to go to law school. However, I wasn't ready to go right on. I am still paying off my student loans. I thought I would give teaching a try before heading off to law school. Who knows, maybe I'll get "hooked."

Second-year teacher

This same research identifies two different orientations toward this more tentative view of teaching as a career. The first is described as an "exploring orientation," characterized by persons who want to try out teaching, but keep other options open. Explorers are uncertain about how long they will stay, but are open to the possibility that teaching will be a long-term pursuit. The second orientation is the "contributing orientation" characterized by those who see teaching as a way to make a contribution to society. Early career contributors choose to teach before embarking on further education or moving on to another career. Other contributors enter teaching mid-career or as a capstone, seeking a way to gain more satisfaction from their work.

These findings parallel other work that indicates the long-term commitment to one job or even a single career is becoming far less prevalent than in the past. In addition, many women and minorities who would have selected teaching in the past because it was one of few professional opportunities open to them, now have a range of other opportunities.

We have yet to examine what this change in career orientation might mean for the long-term commitment to teach. We do know that it calls for a concerted effort to attract highly qualified individuals and then support them so that they are retained in higher numbers and are successful in their work.

Motivations to teach are usually pursued in the initial interviews with prospective candidates. In hiring teachers, it is important to look for those who are highly motivated to make a difference or to give back to their communities. However, even those who are less altruistically motivated can be encouraged and supported in their induction experience so that they deepen their commitments and see what a positive difference they are able to make in the lives of their students.

TEACHER COLLABORATION

Teaching, once regarded as an isolating occupation in which individual teachers worked quite autonomously behind their classroom doors, is becoming more collegial, drawing on the teacher's own instincts and motivations to work in a collaborative environment. Teachers are beginning to work more closely with one another in communities of practice. Induction programs offer one way of helping to connect teachers with one another, to initiate deep, rich conversations about practice and about student learning.

My first-year mentor was incredible. She showed me how to set up the classroom, develop lessons, use rubrics, and gave me many teaching tips. When I was getting ready for the first parent conferences, she came in and helped me get everything in order. She has become a real friend.

Second-year teacher

Formalizing the induction experience has given teachers the permission to admit to the novice status, and to legitimately seek help from others, where in the past they may have felt hesitant to do so. This is more consistent with other professions, which stage levels of responsibilities and hold different expectations of the more experienced professional.

The induction period for teachers has often been compared to a residency period in the medical profession, where novices see their own patients, but work under the guidance of the more experienced doctors. The experienced in the field take responsibility for nurturing and developing the talents of those who will follow them. This sets the stage for a highly consultative practice that characterizes the profession.

The new model of teaching is moving in this direction. It requires that teachers work together to address the learning of students, learn from one another, and problem solve together. It requires that experienced play a role in nurturing and developing the teachers of the future.

THE TEACHING CONTEXT

Induction planners need to consider not only the *act* of beginning teaching, but the *context* in which new teachers learn and perfect their craft once they begin to teach. Teachers begin to teach in a particular setting. Generic knowledge and skills learned in coursework, fieldwork, and student teaching must now be applied to the new context in which they work.

The context of today's multicultural schools is the starting point for a large number of beginning teachers. Yet the vast majority of teachers come from a white, middle-class background. Therefore the cultural gap between children in the schools and the teachers is large and growing.

Preparation to teach in diverse settings is addressed in a number of ways in the teacher's initial preparation. However, knowledge about diversity does not always lead to practices that are effective with diverse groups of students. Sleeter (2001) states that we have concentrated our efforts primarily on the *preparation* of teachers who can teach well in schools serving communities that have been historically underserved. She argues for giving more "attention to what actually happens in classrooms when graduates of teacher preparation programs begin to teach. It is here that the fruits of our efforts has the most impact and there that we as teacher educators need to devote our energies" (p. 102). This argues for more focus on extending that preparation into the induction years.

While all new teachers face particular contextual challenges in beginning to teach, more of these discouraging factors seem to be concentrated and combined in the urban setting. The biggest cultural mismatch between teachers and students is found in our urban schools. New teachers are assigned in high numbers to what are often considered the least-desirable schools. They often work in old, deteriorating facilities and have fewer instructional resources and access to technology than their neighbors in the suburban schools. Schools tend to be unusually large in urban areas, creating a more impersonal environment. Because of the high turnover of teachers in urban schools, it is often difficult to find enough experienced teachers to mentor and support the new teachers at their own site. There is also a high turnover in administrators, further eroding strong support or leadership for change and improvement.

Beginning a teaching career in any context is challenging for the new teacher. However, some contexts are particularly challenging for the novice. Despite the fact that urban schools present a myriad of challenges, teachers do choose to begin their work in an urban setting.

> I want to be part of the solution. This is where I live and I want to give back to my community. It's hard and it's always challenging. I love the kids. That's what keeps me going.
>
> Second-year teacher

A carefully designed support system for the urban educator can ignite the passion for teaching in the hearts and minds of these new educators. The same motivations that enticed them into that setting can help them overcome the discouraging factors and lead them to help today's urban children learn well, stay safe, and graduate by meeting high standards.

OTHER CHALLENGING CONTEXTS

The urban context is not the only challenging context for new teachers. Nor is it the only setting that will present the challenges of working with diverse student populations and students who are English-language learners. All teachers will need to be able to meet the needs of the particular students they serve.

Other geographical contexts present special challenges for new teacher recruitment and support. It is often to recruit and retain teachers to isolated, rural areas and in specific content areas where there continues to be a teacher shortage—such as special education, math, and science.

Rural areas present their own, and sometimes different challenges for teacher recruitment and retention than the urban setting. Rural schools, especially those in impoverished areas, are not always considered ideal places to live by new teachers. Teachers often feel isolated and lack the social and cultural opportunities more readily available in major metropolitan areas. Rural area teachers may feel disconnected from professional colleagues and lack the range of professional development opportunities found elsewhere. The limited number of teachers may mean that the teacher has to teach multiple classes or areas outside of their preparation.

The field of special education, where shortage of well-qualified teachers remains high and the attrition rate exceeds that of general educators, brings its own set of challenges for new teachers. It is a challenging field that continues to lack enough qualified teachers to fill the positions available, so teachers often begin with little or no preparation for this often physically demanding and emotionally draining work. Special education teachers often work in regular school settings, where they may be one of few special education teachers on site. The lack of experienced colleagues nearby leads to a lack of good mentors and role models for these teachers.

There is also a growing resentment by other educators of the "encroachment" of special education into general funding streams, sometimes putting a strain on collegial relationships with general education teachers and administrators. Another source of strained relationships is the push for inclusion of special needs students into general education settings. Not all general education faculty welcome this challenge, and some will even actively resist, increasing the anxiety and frustrations of the new teacher, who wants the best for her students. The increased emphasis on all teachers to collaborate in helping students with disabilities succeed in the general curriculum places demands on general and special educators alike.

These are limited examples of teaching contexts that may provide particular challenges for the beginning teacher. Teachers are beginning a career in a specific context that needs to be considered in any induction experience. Teachers need to come to understand how to be successful as a teacher in the context in which they work.

Preparation programs help teachers understand how to work in a variety of contexts, settings, and grade levels. However, by its very definition, induction becomes particular. Teachers are inducted into a particular role in a particular setting with a particular group of students. Induction programs need to help teachers understand and be effective in the context in which they work.

TEACHER MOTIVATIONS AND INDUCTION PLANNING

Teacher motivations are important to consider in planning for their induction. The plan for effective induction actually begins with the recruitment highly motivated, talented individuals who want to make a contribution. The key to recruiting and retaining the new, altruistically motivated and often highly talented new teachers is to make sure they experience success and are able to make the contributions that enticed them into teaching. The support provided in an induction experience is designed to present the positive challenges and rewards of teaching and to keep teachers from becoming disillusioned.

Among all teachers, whatever their motivation, preparation, or career path to teaching, the initial years are the most crucial. The induction experience is too important to ignore. A good beginning experience not only makes a difference in the retention of new teachers but also shapes their practice in many positive ways and puts them on the path to high-quality teaching.

Those who plan and deliver induction programs need to consider that not all new teachers will remain as active professionals. In fact, systematic attention to these entry years in an induction program may also help identify individuals who are not well suited for the profession early in their careers, so that they can be encouraged to pursue other career options. It is much better to remove those teachers from the classroom early in their careers rather than to let them continue year after year.

A PLANNED INDUCTION PERIOD FOR ALL BEGINNING TEACHERS

The support and mentoring that occur in a well-designed induction program are not a substitute for strong academic preparation, but an adjunct to and extension of that preparation. While the entry period represents the time at which teachers are most vulnerable for leaving, it is also the time in which professional norms and practices can be shaped for a career of lifelong practice and professional development. New teachers need guidance during this period, rather than being left to fend for themselves. Teaching is a complex activity that develops over time, and that the concerns, practices, and views of teachers change during the course of their careers.

Support strategies focused solely on retention miss the opportunity to raise the bar for new teachers. Findings from the California studies of induction demonstrate that teachers that are well supported and mentored are more effective earlier in their careers and move more quickly from survival to success (Bartell, 1995). Classroom knowledge and expertise that is the foundation of the reflective, rich, teaching practice required for today's schools are most effectively fostered and developed in close collaboration with colleagues. The most effective induction programs will focus on more than the "survival level" of teacher development; they will quickly move teachers along the continuum of teacher development to expert practice and to high-quality teaching.

It is this growing knowledge about teacher retention, the attainment of professional competence and the importance of the defining early years that have encouraged increase attention to the induction experience. The induction period, in which the initial introduction of novice teachers to the norms and responsibilities of the profession occurs, is a crucial period that is too important for state policies to ignore and for local schools to allow to occur haphazardly.

The growth of interest in teacher induction is evident in the rapid expansion of programs and state policies since the early 1980s. In early 1984, eight states reported having policies related to beginning teacher support. Two decades later, twenty-eight states had instituted teacher induction policies and funded programs at some level (NASDTEC, 2002) and many have developed standards or expectations to guide this specific period of development for teachers (Interstate New Teacher Assessment and Support Consortium, 1992). Nationally, 55% of new public school teachers report participating in some kind of induction program (Darling-Hammond, 1997).

We have learned much about the benefits of high-quality, standards-driven induction that includes mentoring, assessment, and professional development from a more than a decade of research in California (Bartell, 1995; Olebe, 2001a). These benefits include

- Higher retention of beginning teachers.
- Increased levels of professional efficacy and satisfaction.
- Improved teacher performance.
- Earlier identification of weak teachers for assistance or termination.
- More consistent use of instructional practices that lead to higher levels of student achievement.
- More varied and more complex instructional practices being used by teachers.
- Improved ability of new teachers to engage in reflective practice and critical examination of their work.
- Establishment of professional norms of collegiality and expectations for continued learning.

These early years present an opportunity to shape practice in a way that leads to success for teachers and for their students. We owe it to our new teachers and their students to put our time, energies, and resources to work supporting all of our new teachers during this crucial entry period. Our efforts will pay off in the long run in retention and improved teacher performance.

MEETING THE NEEDS DURING A PLANNED INDUCTION PERIOD

New teachers have specific needs that stem from their novice status. They need to become familiar with their own school and district procedures. They need to learn how to manage their classrooms and to keep appropriate records. They need help with the psychological adjustments related to the demands and stress of the job. They have many needs in the area of curriculum and instruction, and in knowing what to teach and how to best teach it to their own students. They need to learn the norms and practices of their profession. They need to understand and be able to relate to the lives and cultures represented in their classroom. They need to know how to navigate the politics of the school in which they work and the broader context that influences the profession.

Exhibit 1.1 gives examples of the needs in each of these categories. The most effective and comprehensive programs consider this range of needs and recognize that not all teachers need the same kind or level of support and assistance in every area. Too often, the plan for induction is narrowly focused on a limited number of these categories. This book presents a model of induction planning that is comprehensive in scope and gives attention to the range of new teacher needs.

It also presents induction that is highly individualized and differentiated to the individual teacher's particular stage of development and grounded in the teacher's particular classroom context. It is a model of induction that focuses not only on survival and retention, but on success

Exhibit 1.1 New Teacher Needs Addressed in Induction Programs

Category	Examples
Procedural	Familiarity with school and district procedures and expectations for personnel
Managerial	Classroom management strategies; time management; setting up the classroom; getting materials and supplies; scheduling; taking attendance; grading practices; keeping records
Psychological	Managing stress, gaining self-confidence; handling challenges and disappointments; transitioning from student to teacher role; attending to physical and emotional well-being
Instructional	Grade-level curriculum standards and expectations; lesson planning; instructional resources; assessing student progress and using results to shape instruction; using a variety of instructional practices; adapting instruction to meet individual student needs
Professional	Teaching norms and practices; appropriate boundaries and relationships between faculty and students; legal issues; the role of professional organizations; professional development opportunities
Cultural	Developing rapport with students and parents; understanding and appreciating environment; using community resources; valuing diversity; developing cultural proficiency
Political	Getting to know colleagues; contributing to extracurricular program; building relationships with colleagues, staff, and administrators; understanding the broader context of teaching and reform efforts

and the development high-quality teaching. It is a model driven by standards and expectations for what teachers are expected to know and be able to do to foster student success.

IMPLICATIONS FOR PRACTICE

The main points of this chapter and their implications for practice can be summarized as follows:

1. Large numbers of new teachers coming into the teaching force will need to be prepared to teach a more demanding curriculum and be held accountable for results.

2. Learning to teach is a lifelong process; induction is an important phase of development in this process.

3. The induction period, or the first one to three years of teaching, is a time when new teachers should be carefully and systematically introduced to their roles as professionals and into the settings in which they will work.

4. Teachers enter the profession from a variety of preparation routes and bring differing levels of preparation to their initial teaching experience.

5. An effective plan for support of new teachers recognizes and builds on the knowledge and experience the beginning teacher brings to the classroom, assists the teacher in gaining what is weak or lacking, and extends learning so that the teacher moves to higher levels of accomplished teaching.

6. Those working with new teachers should understand what motivates new teachers so they can help new teachers realize their goals for themselves and for their students.

7. Teachers working in particularly challenging contexts, such as urban settings, need to be fully supported in responding to the challenges presented.

8. A planned induction program during the early years helps to retain beginning teachers, improve their performance, and establish habits of practice that lead to career-long development.

9. Teacher needs that should be addressed during the induction period fall into the following categories:
   • Procedural
   • Managerial
   • Psychological
   • Instructional

- Professional
- Cultural
- Political

FOR FURTHER READING

Kane, P. R. (Ed.). (1991). *The first year of teaching: Real world stories from America's teachers.* New York: Walker and Company.
Vivid accounts of beginning teachers, written by new teachers themselves, present a glimpse into the realities of the classroom—the fears and pleasures, the disappointments and the satisfactions. More than 400 teachers submitted accounts of their first-year experience in a national competition and these were the poignant stories selected for sharing.

McDonald, R. E., & Healy, S. (1999). *A handbook for beginning teachers* (2nd ed.). Boston, MA: Addison-Wesley.
This book is offers a practical and rich collection of ideas for new teachers. It presents a day-to-day look at the responsibilities of teaching with a focus on student learning. It includes material about how to design learning objectives, organize subject matter, plan lessons, group students for instruction, evaluate student work, and communicate with parents.

Portner, H. (2002). *Being mentored: A guide for protégés.* Thousand Oaks, CA: Corwin.
The author focuses on being a proactive, receptive protégé that is open to the help provided by a mentor. Topics discussed include
- Building trust and clarifying communication.
- Identifying who does what.
- Learning from watching.
- Deciding where to focus your efforts.
- Planning your professional growth.

Warner, J., & Bryan, C. (1995). *The unauthorized teacher's survival guide.* Indianapolis, IN: Park Avenue Publications.
This book is a very practical guide to the everyday aspects of teaching. It includes advice on how to handle the first day on the job, fit in with staff, develop rapport with students, maintain classroom control, prepare for substitutes, and manage time. There is even a chapter devoted to helping teachers decipher all of the "buzz words" used by educators.

2

Understanding the Stages of Teacher Development

Those who work with new teachers should understand how their skills develop over time. In most views of teacher development, induction emerges as an important stage that presents specific challenges and learning needs for teachers. However, induction cannot be considered in isolation because it is part of a continuum of development that occurs over a career of teaching. This development takes place in a specific context that shapes teacher perceptions and the practice of teaching. This chapter explores the stages of teacher development with a special focus on the induction period as a distinct and crucial stage in the learning-to-teach continuum.

FROM PREPARATION TO PRACTICE

At one time it was assumed that teachers would become fully qualified to teach by virtue of what they had learned in their university preparation programs and that no further learning would be required. We now understand the complexity of teaching expertise as it develops over time and recognize that even well-prepared beginning teachers are still novices and have much to learn.

Even those teachers who have the advantage of excellent preparation are merely well-prepared beginners. These novices bring enthusiasm and a broad understanding of the field and their place in it. They bring knowledge of what is to be taught. They bring a perspective on teaching and learning and some ideas about how to realize that vision in the classroom. They bring an understanding of students and models of teaching practice that they have observed in their own schooling and in their preparation programs. They bring entry-level knowledge about a difficult and complex job.

> The area in which I need more knowledge is in knowing what in the curriculum is most important and must be taught more thoroughly and what is can be given less time. I have everything I need except years of experience that would help me focus on what really needs to be taught.
>
> First-year teacher

We know that it is necessary to channel and direct this enthusiasm while we give new teachers time to more fully develop and shape their practice. New teachers continue to develop as they encounter students with a variety of needs, adapt to new curriculum, and find new ways to ensure that each of their students are learning. Teachers come to a deeper understanding of the learning process as they try to meet the needs of a variety of students in a variety of contexts. Over time, they develop a fuller understanding of the complexity and nuances of teaching and student learning.

CONTINUED LEARNING

Policies in many states now recognize the need for teachers to continue to learn. The old "lifetime credential" that was once given to teachers when they completed a program of studies is becoming quite rare. Most states now require that teachers participate in professional development and renewal activities to keep their credential active. More recent state policies have begun to address the induction phase as an important and distinct learning period. These policies related to teacher certification recognize that good teachers need to keep on learning if they are going to be effective.

Contemporary school reform efforts also recognize the importance of professional development as a crucial part of the implementation plan. When new curricular materials or a new instructional approach is adopted by a school or district, that adoption often includes a training component to help all teachers, even experienced veterans, successfully implement the new approaches. Curriculum planners know that implementation is highly dependent upon the understanding and the ability of the classroom teacher to implement the new approach.

New research on teaching and learning continues to help even the best teachers hone and develop their skills and their practice, adapt to new curricular and instructional approaches, and work with a wide variety of students. Learning to teach, like learning in many other professions, is a lifelong process. Mager (1992) suggests that

> to "become a teacher" might be better thought of as the continuous experience of an individual through which the image of self-as-teacher is formed and refined, and during which knowledge, skills, and values appropriate to the work of teaching, as it is to be practiced in a particular context, are acquired and used. (p. 6)

TEACHING AS A PROFESSION

Continued learning is the mark of most professions. As teaching increasingly becomes more professionalized, we look to other professions for models of practice. We know that many other professionals continue to perfect their craft. Even the most talented musician keeps practicing in order to remain fresh and to learn new repertoire. The computer scientist must keep up with advancing technologies. The physician remains up-to-date on medications and treatments.

The teaching profession departs from some of these other professions, however, in the way newcomers are treated. In many other professions, the assumption of responsibilities is staged so that entry-level professionals gradually acquire a range of skills and assume more advanced assignments along the way. This is not so in the teaching profession. New teachers are typically expected to perform all the same tasks as the more experienced, seasoned professionals from their very first day on the job.

What we are learning about the development of teaching is helping us to recognize the importance of giving special attention to the entry period. A well-planned induction period allows new teachers have the same opportunity as many other professionals have to experience a phased introduction to the responsibilities of the profession. While novices will probably continue to be assigned the same responsibilities as the experienced teacher, a support system to help the new teacher gain skills and to apply practices can help to provide that transition from student to teacher.

Teachers have different needs at different stages of their careers, but those who are truly professional are always seeking new ideas, learning better ways of helping all children learn, and continuing to grow professionally. A better understanding of the characteristics of stages of development can help us provide the kind of assistance that is needed when it is most appropriate for the developing teacher.

TEACHER CAREER STAGES

Most teachers are familiar with stage theory as it applies to child and adolescent development. However, a few early stage theorists suggested that growth and development does not end at adulthood, but continues throughout the life cycle. Erikson (1963; 1982) was a pioneer in exploring first the stages of child and adolescent development, and later extended his work to look at stages of adult development.

Question: What are your concerns as you think about beginning a teaching career?

Response:

- What is the district grading policy? May I change this to fit my needs?
- What is the classroom management philosophy of the district?
- Is there a specific format for lesson plans that I have to follow? Is it compatible with what I have learned?
- What will I have in the way of after school duties? Lunch duties?
- Will I be able to attend workshops of conferences?
- What support is available to me as a new teacher?
- What will the parents be like? Will they support me?
- Will I have all the materials and resources I need?
- Will I be able to handle the students?
- Will I be able to help them learn what is expected?

Preservice teacher

Others have extended the work on human development to an exploration of career development, forming the basis for educational researchers who wanted to understand the life and career development of teachers. Fuller's (1969) early work on teacher development focused on teacher concerns as a way of defining stages of development. She classified developmental levels of concerns in three broad areas: (a) self or survival concerns; (b) management or task concerns; and (c) impact concerns. Her work demonstrated that it is very natural for beginning teachers to focus first on their own survival. As soon as they become more comfortable with their new responsibilities, the students, and the setting, teachers are ready to give more consideration of the task at hand and on a broader range of management issues. Fuller's goal was to support and nurture beginning teachers in ways that would help move them beyond concerns about how they themselves were performing to concerns about the level of impact of their actions on students, parents, colleagues, and the profession.

Fuller's model influenced many other stage theorists who followed and continued to focus on teacher concerns over time. Veenman (1984) identified key concerns of first-year teachers as being disciplining students, motivating them, dealing with individual differences of their students, assessing students' work, relating to parents, organizing class work, and obtaining materials and supplies.

In 1970s and 1980s, a number of other theorists sought to define stages of growing expertise exhibited by teachers. Early stage theorists felt that teachers move through the same series of stages in a rather deterministic way and that the stages are relatively fixed. Each stage of development was considered to be more advanced than the earlier stage, beginning with initial survival and leading to the mature, highly competent teacher. For example, Katz (1979) named the stages of teacher development as follows: (a) survival, (b) consolidation, (c) renewal, and (d) maturity. Similarly, Burden (1980) identified three stages: (a) survival, (b) adjustment, and (c) mature.

Other theorists have looked at how teachers approach their work at various points or phases of their careers. For example, Feiman-Nemser (1983) was among the first to trace teacher development through the pre-training phase (early influences), preservice phase, induction phase, and inservice phase (on-the-job learning). She noted that teacher needs differ during each phase and that we have an opportunity to influence and shape teacher development in different ways at each phase.

Extending and expanding this earlier work, Fessler and Christiansen (1992) present a comprehensive model that emerged from their own review of the literature on teacher development and their own interviews of teachers. They labeled and defined eight stages of their *Teacher Career Cycle Model*: (a) preservice, (b) induction, (c) competency building, (d) enthusiastic and growing, (e) career frustration, (f) career stability, (g) career wind-down, and (h) career exit. Exhibit 2.1 summarizes the key features of each of these stages.

These authors find that teachers exhibit different attitudes about their work at each stage and have thus have different professional development needs. Their needs and their interests are related to the stage of development and they are more receptive to professional development that fits most closely with their needs.

Each of these stages is considered to be flexible and dynamic rather than fixed. A teacher may move back to an earlier stage temporarily or skip a stage entirely. The authors also recognize that a variety of internal and external factors can influence movement from one stage to another.

Fessler and Christiansen, along with other stage theorists, anticipate that a better understanding of the typical stages of development among teachers will help to target professional development activities to meet their needs. For example, an "enthusiastic and growing" teacher may be ready to be trained to assume a role as a mentor of other teachers, whereas

Exhibit 2.1 Teacher Career Stages

Career Stage	Definition
Preservice	The initial professional preparation to teach, whether it be in a college or university or in an alternative program. This phase could also include retraining for a new teaching role.
Induction	The first several years of employment when the teacher is socialized into the norms and expectations of the school and the profession. The teacher may also experience an induction phase when the teacher moves to a new grade level or a new school setting.
Competency building	The teacher strives to improve teaching skills and abilities and to build a repertoire of teaching strategies.
Enthusiastic and growing	The teacher has reached a high level of competency but enthusiastically continues to learn and progress as a professional.
Career frustration	The teacher experiences disillusionment and waning job satisfaction. This is often described as "teacher burnout."
Career stability	The teacher has reached a career plateau and does little more than what is expected. This stage is sometimes characterized by disengagement and stagnation.
Career wind-down	The teacher prepares to leave the profession, reflecting back on their career.
Career exit	The teacher leaves the job and transitions to retirement or to another career.

Source: Adapted from Fessler, R., & Christiansen, J. (1992). *The teacher career cycle: Understanding and guiding the professional development of teachers.* Boston: Allyn & Bacon.

such a role would be inappropriate for a struggling new teacher or for a teacher who was focused on moving toward retirement and career exit. A person at the "career stability" stage could possibly be rejuvenated if given a new teaching assignment or some different responsibilities. Teachers getting ready to exit might need to receive guidance in how to plan for their retirement years.

THE DEVELOPMENT OF TEACHING EXPERTISE

A somewhat different perspective of teacher development can be found in the work of Berliner (1994). His theories take us beyond the "teacher

Exhibit 2.2 Levels of Teaching Expertise

Level	Categorization	Characteristics
Stage 1. Novice level	Deliberate	Novices are learning the commonplaces and some context-free rules of teaching. This is the stage for learning objective facts and features of situations. Gaining experience seems more important than verbal information to the novice.
Stage 2. Advanced beginner level	Insightful	Experience becomes melded with verbal knowledge and episodic and case knowledge is accumulated. Similarities across contexts are recognized. Experience affects behavior, but the advanced beginner may still have no sense of what is important.
State 3. Competent level	Rational	Teachers make conscious choices about what they are going to do. They set goals and priorities, plan, and choose sensible means for reaching the ends they have in mind. They are able to determine what is important and what is not. They learn to make curriculum and instruction decisions.
Stage 4. Proficient level	Intuitive	Intuition or know-how becomes prominent. Teachers are able to holistically assess the situation and recognize common patterns. They draw on their rich case knowledge.
Stage 5. Expert level	Arational	Experts have both an intuitive grasp of the situation and seem to sense in nonanalytic and nondeliberative ways the appropriate response to be made. They act fluidly and effortlessly.

Source: Adapted from Berliner, D.C. (1994). The wonders of exemplary performance. In J. N. Mangieri & C. C. Block (Eds.), *Creating powerful thinking in teachers and students*. Fort Worth: Harcourt Brace.

concerns" model and focus us on the cognitive processes of teachers—how teachers think about and describe their work. He found that teachers think differently at different stages in their development.

Berliner describes five levels of development: novice, advanced beginner, competent, proficient, and expert. At each successive stage, teachers develop their teaching repertoire and think about their own teaching in more complex ways. The stages are described in Exhibit 2.2.

Those who seek to help teachers advance along this continuum of development need to provide appropriate learning activities, rich dialogue and discussion, and critical and thoughtful discussions of teaching practice. Induction programs that focus only on survival do little to move the teacher beyond the novice stage. While these needs cannot be ignored, induction programs should be focused on more than beginning teacher concerns and survival-level strategies. Once teachers have developed such strategies, continued learning should move them beyond the survival level and along the continuum to teaching expertise.

Few teachers will become expert in their early years. However, beginning teachers need to see models of expert teaching and be given opportunities to develop in ways that will encourage expertness as an eventual, long-term goal. To help us understand what he means by expertness, Berliner (1994) suggests eight propositions:

1. Experts excel mainly in their own domain and in a particular context.

2. Experts often develop automaticity for the repetitive operations that are needed to accomplish their goal.

3. Experts are more sensitive to the task demands and social situation when solving problems.

4. Experts are more opportunistic and flexible in their teaching than are novices.

5. Experts represent problems in qualitatively different ways than do novices.

6. Experts have fast and accurate pattern-recognition capabilities. Novices cannot always make sense of what they experience.

7. Experts perceive meaning patterns in the domain in which they are experienced.

8. Experts may begin to solve problems slower, but they bring richer and more personal sources of information to bear on the problem that they are trying to solve. (pp. 167-180)

This view of teacher development is consistent with the work of many leaders in the field (Shulman, 1987; Liebermann, 1988; Darling-Hammond, 1997) who have written about teaching as a complex, dynamic, interactive, intellectual activity, as opposed to one that is characterized by routine tasks. The complexity and nuances of teaching take time to develop and master. Expert teachers keep student learning at the center of their work and continue to reflect on ways to help all students reach their full potential. They react almost automatically based on cues and nuances that the less-expert teacher might not notice. They know intuitively when students are puzzled or perplexed. They understand what each student needs to move ahead in the student's learning. They know how much of a challenge to present and when to present it. They know a variety of ways to present subject matter to their students and persist until it is understood. It is this view of teaching that demands our attention and fuels the work of teacher induction activities. This view of teaching is discussed more fully in Chapter 6, which focuses on a vision of reflective teaching that is intended to lead to expertise.

STAGE THEORIES AND INDUCTION

In each theory of teacher development presented here, the entry or induction years are a distinct phase with some common characteristics. Exhibit 2.3 outlines the theories discussed here and highlights what could be characterized as the induction phase.

Exhibit 2.3 The Induction Years as Defined in Stage Theories of Teacher Development

Fuller	Katz	Burden	Feiman-Nemser	Fessler and Christiansen	Berliner
			Pretraining		
			Preservice	Preservice	
Self or survival concerns	Survival	Survival	Induction	Induction	Novice
Management or task concerns	Consolidation	Adjustment		Competency building	Advanced beginner
	Renewal	Mature	Inservice	Enthusiastic and growing	Competent
Impact concerns	Maturity				
					Proficient
				Career frustration	
				Career stability	Expert
				Career wind-down	
				Career exit	

Note: The descriptors of the induction phase in each theory are shaded in gray.

The characterization of the induction phase is fairly consistent across these theories. During the initial years, teachers are novices who have a great deal to learn. They are concerned about surviving on a day-to-day basis. They are focused more on how they themselves are performing than on the performance and progress made by their individual students. They are trying to apply what they have learned in their coursework to their own classrooms and are learning to make adjustments that seem to work for their own students. They are developing a repertoire of strategies, approaches, and techniques that they will begin to rely on over time. They are discarding ideas that don't appear to work for them. They are looking forward to continued learning and development over time.

New teachers have special and unique professional development needs during this phase of development. As outlined in Chapter 1 (Exhibit 1.1), these needs are procedural, managerial, psychological, instructional, professional, cultural, and political.

Those who assist new teachers should not wait until teachers ask for help. Novices are often reluctant to seek help and, even when they do, they may not know what help they actually need. They often misidentify the source of a problem. What they may view as a discipline problem may actually be an instructional issue. Induction programs should recognize the uniqueness of the beginning phases of teaching and be designed to focus specifically on the full range of teacher needs and concerns, those stated and those not stated.

TEACHER DEVELOPMENT IN CONTEXT

Just as student learning is influenced by a variety of factors, teacher learning is impacted conditions that may help or hinder the desired growth.

Many of the later stage theorists recognized that teacher development occurs not in isolation, but within a broader context. This context helps shape the way teachers grow and develop over time. For example, Fessler and Christiansen (1992) place the teacher career cycle into the context of two spheres of influence—personal and organizational factors. The authors point out that factors interact with and influence the teacher's own development. A better understanding of these factors can help induction planners be more attuned to the unique needs of each new teacher.

Some personal factors discussed by these authors include family issues and factors; critical incidents or events; a personal or family crises; individual goals, aspirations, and dispositions; outside interests; and the life stage of the teacher.

For example, a teacher who is reassessing life and her goals after going through a divorce or a death in the family may not have the time or emotional resources to give to growing and learning professionally or to taking on new challenges. Or perhaps she is seeking new challenges. A teacher who is beginning a graduate program to obtain an advanced degree may shift priorities and look beyond his own classroom while he is meeting new expectations as a student himself. Because this is so highly dependent on the individual's own personal reaction to life events and situations, those that are working with and advising teachers in their professional development need to know teachers well and be able to assess what is appropriate for each individual.

Because individual teachers are a part of a larger school organization, with its own norms and culture, development is also impacted by factors in this wider environment. Organizational factors that appear to influence the teacher's development include school bureaucratic regulations; the management style of the school principal; the atmosphere of public trust of education; societal expectations for schools; and the impacts of professional organizations and teacher unions.

> This was really a chaotic place when I first got here. Kids were not getting to classes on time. You would send kids to the office and they would just send them back without doing anything. Now it's really a well-run place. Our principal has made a difference.
>
> Third-year teacher

These organizational factors help to establish the context for teachers' work and can influence their development in a positive or negative way. We know that a teacher may be successful in one setting, but not in another. For teachers who believe that they lack support from their administrator, parents, or the public, the entry period is that much more difficult. Teachers who believe that the school is an insurmountable bureaucracy that they do not understand can easily become disillusioned. These and other contextual factors can serve as a powerful incentive or disincentive to the new teacher.

When teachers accept that first teaching assignment, they are entering a profession in the broad sense, but they are also taking a position in a particular organization. That organization will be perceived by the teacher as supportive of their work and their continued learning, or unsupportive and frustrating. The organizational context in which teachers began their work will shape their views of teaching and of the profession in a very real, and sometimes lasting, sense.

Those who work with new teachers need to consider not only how new teachers move through the typical stages of development, but how this development can be influenced by the context. A positive context can actually be used as a part of the support structure. A context that is not so positive can perhaps be shaped or reshaped to offer a more supportive environment.

THE INDUCTION STAGE

A common thread that runs through the work on stages of teacher development is the distinct identification of an entry period that has the potential to shape professional practice for the rest of the teacher's career. The induction phase is often a "make or break" point for the teacher, as evidenced by the traditionally high dropout rate during these initial years.

As pointed out in Chapter 1, the induction stage is typically considered to span the first three years of teaching. During this period, teachers begin to try out a number of strategies and approaches to see what works and what doesn't work. They are beginning to learn about the characteristics of the students they are teaching and what they can be expected to do. They are learning what is to be taught and beginning to experiment with ways to teach that curriculum to their students. As early stage theorists noted, the terms *survival* and *discovery* are apt descriptions of this period in the teacher's life.

Survival appears to be an appropriate characterization of the initial struggles in which most new teachers engage. They are stressed, tired, and often find it difficult to keep up. They often stay just one day, and sometimes only one period, ahead of their students. They have difficulty managing the basic paperwork required of teachers (grading, reports, etc.) and are trying to find a classroom management style that works for them. They are often intimidated by demanding parents and administrators.

I have four preps every day and I see about 180 kids each day. I think I am just scrambling for time. First there were the five-week report cards, then the Stanford 9 testing the next week. All my own portfolio work has to be finished by May. So things are pretty hectic and I have no social life.

First-year teacher

Many learn to navigate those entry years, with or without support, and go on to become highly productive teachers. However, too many new teachers fail to survive. We know that the initial years are the period in which the teacher is most at risk for leaving the profession. More of those teachers might have survived this early period if given appropriate support and assistance.

Discovery is another appropriate characterization of the induction stage. There is so much to learn and discover as the new teacher shapes his or her own practice in the context of the classroom as learning laboratory. New teachers learn that some lessons work and some do not. And some lessons work with some of the students but not with others.

New teachers also discover what their students are capable of doing and what is beyond their initial level of understanding. They think of new ways of presenting the concepts to be taught when the first approach is not successful. They get to know their students and what motivates and challenges them. They apply what they studied in the preparation programs and only now begin to fully understand the connections between theory and practice.

> I love it. Basically I'm hooked. I think because of the kids. The subjects I teach are fun, too, and I love the fact that we're able to discover things together and learn together.
>
> First-year teacher

This early and crucial discovery period is one that needs careful attention by policy makers, school administrators, and teacher-leaders. The induction period need not be a period of lonely struggle and complete disillusionment, but with the appropriate support, one that leads very naturally and positively to the more advanced stages of teacher development and, ultimately, to expert teaching.

BRIDGING PREPARATION AND PRACTICE

A common metaphor used to describe the induction stage is that of a bridge. The induction period provides that a crucial link between formal preparation and expert practice. However, traversing that bridge is not always a simple matter.

Beginning teachers often experience a conflict between their ideal view of teaching and their actual experience with teaching. Armed with all the new theories and ideas about learning, new teachers often encounter different philosophies and practices than they were exposed to in their preparation programs (Huling-Austin, 1992; Huling-Austin, Odell, Ishler, Kay, & Edelfelt, 1989). It is difficult for new teachers to strike out in a different direction than that of established practices in their school. In fact, schools are very traditional places that often discourage innovation by individual teachers, particularly new teachers.

Behaviors of beginning teachers are not always consistent with their expressed beliefs. New teachers are quite idealistic about what they will be able to accomplish and how students will respond. Beginning teachers know they should modify their instruction and respond to each child's learning needs. Yet, their need to maintain control of the class as a group keeps them from seeing their students as individual learners.

This early experience can lead to disillusionment and early burnout on the part of the new teacher. Most of the research on teacher retention identifies the first five years as the period in which teachers are most likely to leave the profession. Gold (1996) conducted an extensive review of the literature and identified the following factors as potential sources of teacher disillusionment:

- Negative work-related factors
- Student violence and discipline problems
- Insensitivity of the administration
- Parents who are unreasonable and/or unconcerned
- Criticism from the public
- Excessive paperwork and demanding workload
- Lack of promotional opportunities
- A negative workplace environment
- Role conflict and role ambiguity
- Marriage and family relationships
- Personality characteristics

A strong program of support and assistance can mitigate much of the stress related to these factors during the crucial early years. A supportive induction program that can anticipate some of these stress producers can help teachers through these challenging early years so that they are successful and are more likely to be retained in the profession.

Too often those supporting new teachers want every teacher to succeed, even those who should not be in the classroom. Some individuals are simply ill suited for the challenge of teaching or for their particular assignment. A strong induction program should make possible the early identification of these individuals so that they can be counseled early to pursue a different career or to perhaps to work in a different setting or at a different grade level.

PSYCHOLOGICAL STAGES
FOR THE FIRST-YEAR TEACHER

Among the early years of teaching, the first year is often thought to be the most challenging for the newcomer. Moir (1999) traced the development of the new teachers as they move through the vulnerable first year of teaching from a psychological standpoint. Her work demonstrates how teachers begin with high hopes in *anticipation* and a somewhat romanticized view of teaching. They quickly become overwhelmed and move to a *survival* phase, struggling to keep up. They become very focused on the day-to-day aspects of teaching. That phase often leads to *disillusionment,* and teachers may begin to question both their commitment and their competence. The

Exhibit 2.4   Phases in the First Year of Teaching

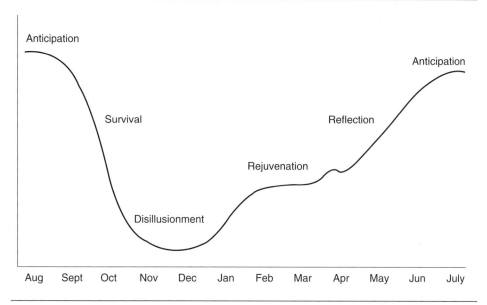

Source: Moir, E. (1999). Used with permission.

duration and intensity of this phase can vary. After a winter break, they typically return rested and relaxed and will enter a period of gradual *rejuvenation*. During this phase, they gain confidence and develop new coping strategies. Toward the end of the school year, they enter a period of *reflection* as they look back on the year and are able to appreciate their successes and think about what they might do differently in the coming year. (See Exhibit 2.4).

Understanding the emotional state of mind that teachers during this crucial first year helps to provide the kind of support needed in a timely manner. Teachers will not often express their concerns, for fear of appearing to be incompetent and unable to cope. If support providers can anticipate what teachers may be experiencing, they can help surface these concerns and reassure teachers at the appropriate times. Moir (1999) writes that "recognizing the stages that new teachers go through gives us a framework within which we can begin to design support programs to make the first year of teaching a more productive experience for our new colleagues" (p. 23).

SCHOOL CONTEXT AND THE BEGINNING TEACHER

While the stage of development is important, other factors impact how teachers form their views of the teaching role during this initial period of development. The school context itself plays a large role in the socialization of the new teacher. Teachers are socialized not only into the norms of the profession, but into the culture and context of the workplace in which they find themselves. A teacher who is a strong contributor and innovator in one context may feel stifled in another. Supportive colleagues, administrators, parents, and the students themselves make a difference in how well the teacher adapts to the setting and to the role of teaching.

A teacher who feels supported by the principal may continue to develop and grow with that support. That same teacher may feel her efforts are thwarted in another context under different administrative leadership or with colleagues who are guided by different norms and expectations that those of the innovating teacher.

Little (1987; 1990) emphasizes the importance of the norms in the school as a workplace and how those expectations shape teacher learning and practice. At some schools, the atmosphere is one that encourages collaboration and sharing among teachers, and in others, teachers stick to themselves and do not share with one another.

My mentor was helpful in giving me ideas. The teacher next door is helpful, but he's new, too. A lot of teachers are into their own work. I'm never comfortable approaching them.

First-year teacher

Some teaching contexts are more difficult than others. Unfortunately, new teachers are often assigned to work in the most challenging settings. They are highly concentrated in urban and in low-performing schools, are assigned to work with students who have many remedial learning needs, are assigned mixed grade-level assignments, and may not have their own permanent classroom.

Chapter 3 includes a more thorough discussion of the importance of the school context and how it can be shaped to more effectively support the new teacher. The context and working conditions in the school context play an important part in not only impacting the morale of the new teacher, but in shaping their long-term views of their students and of themselves as professionals. Beginning teachers must understand and become comfortable in the context in which they are working. Improving these conditions, when possible, will help to develop a supportive environment to nurture positive teacher growth and development and long-term commitment.

A supportive, nurturing context for new teachers benefits all teachers who work in that context. When new teachers are well supported in a context that nurtures and develops professionalism, the entire school becomes a place where teachers and their students thrive and grow.

THE INDUCTION STAGE
AND THE ALTERNATE-ROUTE TEACHER

Most of the work on teacher development and teacher career stages has focused on traditionally prepared teachers who complete their preparation before they begin to take responsibility for their own students in their own classrooms. However, not all teachers begin teaching with a strong professional preparation program to guide them. Increasingly, large numbers of teachers enter teaching through alternate certification routes, bringing differing levels of preparation to their initial work. Some, like Anna (see Chapter 1) have no formal education coursework before they enter the classroom. For these teachers, beginning to teach is even more of a challenge than it is for their more prepared colleagues.

Alternative programs have been developed in response to widespread shortages of teachers across the country, particularly shortages in urban and rural areas, and in specific specialty areas, such as math, science, and special education.

There is much debate about the quality and impact of these alternative programs that most often offer the opportunity for teachers to "learn while they teach." There are probably as many varieties of alternative-preparation programs as there are traditional preparation programs, so it is difficult to generalize about the efficacy of these alternatives. The requirements candidates meet in these programs vary from one state to other. Teachers who enter through alternative routes bring a wide range and differing levels of preparation to their initial teaching experience. Some alternative routes allow individuals to begin with no professional coursework; others come with extensive preparatory work. In most cases, the goal is to eventually earn a credential. The program of studies for the alternate route candidate may or may not be equivalent to the formal academic program offered to the traditional route candidate.

While there are many definitions and varieties of programs that are labeled as "alternate routes," the main characteristic is that, unlike the more traditionally prepared, alternate-route teachers most often complete their initial preparation requirements while they are teaching, often in evening, weekend, or summer programs. They often become the teacher-of-record before they actually have earned an initial teaching credential.

Alternate-route programs have emerged as a way to address existing teacher shortages and are offered by universities as well as a variety of other entities and organizations. Many universities offer both traditional and alternative options for candidates and the programs frequently are very similar in the content presented and the skills taught. When school districts or other authorized entities outside of the university are authorized to offer alternative programs, these programs carry no academic credit, but, if approved by the state certification entity, result in a valid license to practice.

What is most often left out or minimized in the alternative route program is the formal clinical or student teaching experience in the classroom of a more experienced teacher, the experience that traditionally prepared teachers often value most highly (Henry, 1989). Alternate-route teachers often receive some form of mentoring and support by district and/or university supervisors as they begin work in their own classrooms, but they have not had the time to observe and develop with the guided practice that most student teachers receive under the daily guidance of a more experienced classroom teacher for an extended period of time. These teachers often rely heavily on their own experience with teaching and learning, often teaching as they themselves were taught.

There is much debate about the merits of alternative certification programs and the effectiveness of the teachers produced through these programs. However, these options have become a part of the landscape. The shortage of teachers has created a need for this option and a growing number of teachers are entering classrooms in our schools through these alternative routes.

We do know that there is a growing interest among college-educated individuals who want to change careers, embark on second career, or enter teaching after being out of the workforce. We also know that many bright, talented people may be attracted to teaching who may not be able to pursue this goal in a more traditional program of studies that takes them out of the workforce for a year or more. We also know that alternate-route teachers are more likely to be willing to work in hard-to-staff urban schools. Alternative preparation programs also attract more males and a more diverse candidate pool to teaching, enriching the teaching force in important ways (Houston, Marshall, & McDavid, 1993; Feistritzer, 1993).

Despite the benefits and perhaps some positive end results of such alternative programs, few would argue that these individuals are as well prepared as the traditionally prepared teacher when they first enter the classroom. They do not have the same level of understanding as those who have completed all formal academic and professional preparation and have apprenticed under a more experienced teacher for an extended period of time. Like the more traditionally prepared teachers, they are still learning. However, these alternate-route teachers have much more to learn than those who enter teaching at a later point in their learning process.

> *The Alternate-Route Teacher: The teacher who serves as the teacher of record in the classroom without the benefit of having completed an initial preparation program.*

The alternate-route teacher induction needs are especially acute and have not always been well addressed. Unfortunately, these teachers are most often found in highest numbers in our urban schools. Therefore, the least qualified teachers often serve students who have the greatest learning needs.

I attended the [new teacher support] meetings and then I felt that it wasn't intended for me; it seemed to be intended for teachers that have a preliminary credential rather than an emergency permit. Now I believe this year it is more inclusive in that they are trying to include the emergency permit people, but I've been unable to participate with the time pressure of having a three-year-old and being in a credential program and teaching full-time.

Second-year teacher

Because of these differences in preparation levels of novice teachers, the unique needs of alternate-route teachers deserve special attention in the induction period. These teachers do not have the same level of knowledge and understanding as those who enter classrooms with a full academic preparation and guided teaching experiences.

California provides an example of a state with a high number of teachers who enter through alternate routes. The formal alternate-route program is called an "intern program." While interns have demonstrated that they meet a subject-matter requirement and therefore meet the federal definition of "highly qualified," they lack pedagogical and professional preparation.

The state-funded induction program that recently became a required part of the credential structure in California was not designed for the alternate-route teacher. The extensive research on induction in California has been focused on the needs of teachers who enter with the knowledge and skills gained in formal preparation. Now that induction services are being extended to all teachers, program sponsors are expected to adapt the induction plans and activities to these alternate-route teachers. They are expected to stage induction programs to the teacher's appropriate level of readiness at appropriate times in their development. However, it is difficult to provide these teachers with an induction experience that was designed for the fully prepared teacher and is built on some common understandings that were developed in the preservice years.

"Whereas some children are gaining access to teachers who are more qualified and well prepared than in years past, a growing number of poor and minority children are being taught by teachers who are sorely unprepared for the task they face."

Darling-Hammond (2001, p. 771)

Exhibit 2.5 Career Stage Variations for Traditionally Prepared and Alternate-Route Teachers

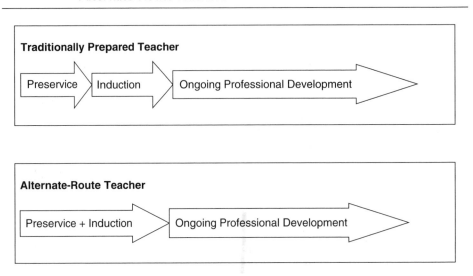

The alternate-route teacher faces all of the same issues and concerns as a fully certified new teacher, but also has additional, and sometimes different, needs. Induction, in this case, is taking place while the teacher is also working on obtaining a full credential, compressing the crucial preparation and induction phases into one phase that can be even more overwhelming for teachers. Alternate-route teachers are still mastering the essential knowledge and skills of a typical preservice curriculum, but they are also faced with the range of induction needs described earlier. Exhibit 2.5 displays the modified view of the career stages for the alternate route teacher, using the categories of Preservice, Induction, and Professional Development as the key phases of teacher development.

Many induction-program sponsors treat the alternate-route teacher very much like the fully prepared new teacher, with little recognition of the differing levels of knowledge, experience, and understanding that teachers bring to their roles. Some induction program sponsors fail to deal with the alternate-route teacher at all in the belief that this teacher seems very much engaged in meeting ongoing course requirements and does not have time to be involved in the induction program. Neither of these approaches seems adequate.

The induction of alternate-route teachers should be addressed in ways that are appropriate to their own readiness and stage of development. As long as there is a shortage of fully prepared teachers in certain subject areas and in certain geographical locations, the alternate-route teacher will continue to impact the lives and learning of many children. While the induction of all teachers is considered in this book, each of the following chapters gives special attention to the challenges of giving support to these often-ignored alternate-route beginning teachers. No matter how or at what point a teacher enters the profession, that teacher needs support that will meet his or her specific needs.

IMPLICATIONS FOR PRACTICE

The main points of this chapter and their implications for practice can be summarized as follows:

1. Teaching is a complex activity that develops over time. Outstanding teachers are always seeking to learn and grow as professionals.

2. Teachers have different needs at different stages of their careers. Professional development should be targeted toward those specific developmental needs.

3. The induction phase is an important part of most stage theories and is a bridge between preparation and practice.

4. During the induction stage, teachers are concerned about day-to-day survival and are focused more on their own performance and actions than on individual students. They are developing their own style and teaching strategies and seek to apply what they have learned and make adjustments to their own classroom situations. Much of what they do is by trial and error.

5. The novice teacher cannot be expected to be as effective as the highly expert teacher. Support can help a teacher in the crucial induction stage.

6. Teacher development is influenced by personal and organizational factors that contribute to the context of teaching. This context must be considered in planning induction programs.

7. The induction period is a crucial period in the teacher's development; appropriate support during this period can help to avoid early teacher burnout.

8. Understanding the psychological stages that the typical first-year teacher experiences can help support providers provide needed assistance at the appropriate times.

9. Teachers begin their work in a specific context. Some contexts present more challenges than others to the beginning teacher. Teachers should be assisted in understanding and working in their own particular context.

10. Alternate-route teachers begin their work with little or no formal preparation to teach. Induction programs are not often designed to accommodate these teachers.

11. All teachers need support that is designed for their specific needs at point of entry and into the initial years.

FOR FURTHER READING

Daloz, L.A. (1999). *Mentor: Guiding the journey of adult learners*. San Francisco: Jossey-Bass.
This book offers new perspectives for understanding adult learners and suggests in concrete and practical ways, based on current developmental theory, how we can work more effectively to improve the quality of their educational experience. The author draws on his own extensive research and experience in working with adult learners.

Joyce, B.R., Showers, B., & Fullan, M.G. (2002). *Student achievement through staff development*, 3rd ed. Alexandria, VA: Association for Supervision and Curriculum Development.
In this update of a now classic book on professional development for teachers, the authors expand on their basic principles of professional development that are designed to enhance professionalism, support instructional improvement, and accelerate student learning. The authors present case studies of successful programs where inquiry is apparent and present a framework for evaluation of programs of professional development.

Vella, J. (2002). *Learning to listen, learning to teach: The power of dialogue in educating adults*. San Francisco: Jossey-Bass.
This book focuses on principles of adult learning and describes a process that can be used by those assisting new teachers. The book is a guide to becoming an effective teacher of adults across cultures through listening, dialogue, and mutual respect. Needs assessment and accountability are also covered in this book.

3

The Characteristics of Effective Induction Programs

Induction is a part of the career-long teacher-development continuum. Care should be taken in developing and implementing induction programs. Support strategies should be individualized to meet new teacher needs, as well as responsive to the context in which the teacher begins to work. This chapter outlines the characteristics of effective induction programs that serve as an impetus to career-long development.

EFFECTIVE INDUCTION PROGRAMS

An effective induction experience helps to retain promising teachers and helps them become more effective. It is important to nurture and develop talent and enthusiasm so that new teachers do not become discouraged, but are encouraged to continue to hone and refine their skills. A formal program of induction helps to acquaint new teachers with the responsibilities of teaching, helps them develop thoughtful practice, and brings them into a professional community that encourages and supports its members.

> It keeps the creative, energetic new teachers in the profession—the ones who are good enough and smart enough to have other options. They don't get discouraged and move to other lines of work.
>
> Induction program director

Because induction programs have been a part of the landscape for more than twenty years, we have learned some things about what makes them effective. This chapter focuses on the key elements of effective induction programs in a variety environments and settings.

THE ORGANIZATION OF EFFECTIVE INDUCTION PROGRAMS

There are many ways to design, organize, and deliver effective induction programs. Programs vary by size of school, district, geographical region, and number of new teachers hired. They are shaped by state policy and by local context and conditions. However, research indicates (Bartell, 1995; Odell & Huling, 2000; Olebe, 2001a; Tushnet, Briggs, Elliot, Esch, Haviland, Humphrey, et al., 1992) that the most successful induction programs include the following key elements:

- Clarity about the purpose and intended outcomes of the program;
- Sufficient attention to leadership and administration of the program;
- Collaboration among organizations, groups, and individuals involved in providing induction services;
- Support of site administrators who are well informed about the purpose and goals of the program;
- An understanding of and linkages with the university preparation program that prepare the teacher for practice;
- Attention to the context in which new teachers are assigned to work and their specific teaching assignments;
- Involvement of experienced teacher mentors who are carefully selected and trained to effectively guide and assist new teachers;
- Provision of scheduled, structured time for experienced and beginning teachers to work together;
- Professional development for new teachers—training that is related to their immediate needs and their current stage of professional development;
- Individual follow-up by experienced educators so that new teachers learn to use new skills effectively in their classrooms;

- Feedback to beginning teachers about their progress in meeting professional goals and expectations; and
- Evaluation of the program and its impact on new teachers and their students.

Together these elements form the basis of a strong plan for inducting the new teacher. Few existing induction programs meet all of these elements consistently for all new teachers in all settings. These key elements are discussed in this chapter.

PROGRAM PURPOSES

Induction programs are designed to accomplish a number of things on behalf of new teachers, their students, and the schools in which they work. Induction program planners that are quite clear and intentional about these purposes will be most likely to galvanize energy and resources toward accomplishing these goals.

State-sponsored systems of teacher induction are often quite specific about program intent. For example, the goals of the California induction system are stated in the enabling legislation.

The system shall do all of the following:

1. Provide an effective transition into the teaching career for first-year and second-year teachers in California.

2. Improve the educational performance of pupils through improved training, information, and assistance for new teachers.

3. Enable beginning teachers to be effective in teaching pupils who are culturally, linguistically, and academically diverse.

4. Ensure the professional success and retention of new teachers.

5. Ensure that a support provider provides intensive individualized support and assistance to each participating beginning teacher.

6. Improve the rigor and consistency of individual teacher performance assessments and the usefulness of assessment results to teachers and decision makers.

7. Establish an effective, coherent system of performance assessments that are based on the California Standards for the Teaching Profession adopted by the commission in January 1997.

8. Examine alternative ways in which the general public and the educational profession may be assured that new teachers who

remain in teaching have attained acceptable levels of professional competence.

9. Ensure that an individual induction plan is in place for each participating beginning teacher and is based on an ongoing assessment of the development of the beginning teacher.

10. Ensure continuous program improvement through ongoing research, development, and evaluation. (California Education Code § 44279.1)

The purposes of the California induction program are similar to induction programs in the other states that have codified their support programs for beginning teachers. As was pointed out in Chapter 1, at least twenty-eight states have established some requirements for induction programs. California's model, one of the longest running and best-established state-sponsored programs, is a model for induction programs elsewhere.

Most states and localities have invested heavily in preparation and recruitment efforts. Improving retention is a way to protect that initial investment of time, energy, and resources. In the current era of accountability, most states also want assurance that these teachers are successful in their work and that students are making progress. Increasingly, states are developing standards or expectations for beginning teachers and ways to assess teachers to ensure that they are meeting those standards as a part of their induction programs. California's model of induction is a standards-driven model that allows for local tailoring and flexibility, making it well suited for the present environment that demands accountability.

Whether a program is state initiated or locally designed, implementation is locally determined. Although state policy makers may have broad policy objectives in mind when a program is created, we know that local program purposes, while often aligned with the state purposes, may differ in emphasis and focus. We know that state plans and purposes often become shaped by local districts to fit their own context. Consider, for example, the goals of one local California Beginning Teacher Support and Assessment (BTSA) Program that are cited in Exhibit 3.1.

The goals of the program need to be made clear to local governing bodies, school leaders, and to all program participants so that everyone is guided by a common set of understandings. These goals will help to drive the design, delivery, and support of programmatic features, the implementation of the program, and the evaluation of the progress that us made. The goals need to be examined on a regular basis to see if modifications are needed. It is important to keep in mind that the ultimate goal of all induction programs should be to achieve teacher and student success.

Exhibit 3.1 Sample BTSA Program Purpose, Mission, and Goals

Purpose
To create and deliver participating teacher-centered quality services that will enhance the academic achievement and overall growth of students.

Mission
Participating teachers in the two-year BTSA Induction Program experience enhanced professional growth and development. They become increasingly competent teachers through a rich and thoughtful process of inquiry and reflection. Each participating teacher gains a professional voice by working in close concert with experienced colleagues and a trained support provider to chart their own progress through the continuum of skills, knowledge, and abilities associated with the *California Standards of the Teaching Profession* (CSTP), state adopted student content standards, State Frameworks, and the *California Formative Assessment and Support System for Teachers* (CFASST).

GOAL ONE
Each participating teacher will create an *Individualized Induction Plan* (IIP) based on a personal professional growth continuum found in the Description of Practice (DOP).

GOAL TWO
Implement and use the *California Formative Assessment and Support System for Teachers* (CFASST) that provides common indicators of progress through the *California Standards of the Teaching Profession*.(CSTP), State Frameworks, and State-adopted Student Content Standards and specific guidance to the participating teacher in his or her own school context.

GOAL THREE
Provide training, assistance, and support to each participating teacher.

GOAL FOUR
Integrate formative assessment indicators into further training and support through ongoing dialogue.

GOAL FIVE
Develop a body of knowledge on induction to professional practice that can be shared among participating member districts for use with participating teachers beyond the limitations of the consortium.

Source: Sacramento BTSA Consortium Web site. Retrieved October 15, 2003 from http://www.btsacacramento.org.

INDUCTION PROGRAM LEADERSHIP

Strong program leadership is essential for an effective induction experience. Some induction programs are organized, managed and delivered at the site level. However, more often they are organized by the district, or even by a consortium of districts, and implemented at the individual school site level. Still others have university leadership and involvement, either as a partner or in playing the primarily leadership role.

Regardless of the organizational and administrative structure, the program needs leadership by an individual or individuals who have that role as a major part of their assignment so that sufficient attention can be paid to operation of the overall program. The larger programs need to devote more leadership time and energy to ensure that there is consistency in program delivery.

Those charged with leadership must be clear about their roles and responsibilities. They should have a view of the goals for the program and a plan for implementing those goals. They need to keep all participants informed about the program plans and implementation schedule. They should ensure that the implementation of the plans is progressing on schedule.

In larger and more complex programs, a leadership team is often selected to attend to the functioning of the program. In this case, the team meets often to plan, confer, and discuss the program direction. All parties understand their roles and responsibilities and keep in contact with one another. They respect the division of responsibility and work together when needed.

A variety of individuals and organizations may be involved in developing programs and providing resources, support, and activities that become a part of the total program. The types of organizations that may be involved include P–12 schools and districts, institutions of higher education, teacher organizations, research firms, parent groups, community organizations, local businesses, and foundations. When multiple individuals or organizations are involved, clear delineation of responsibilities and effective and frequent communication is essential. When many organizations are involved, the efforts need to be coordinated.

The induction program may also draw upon the existing programs and personnel within the district. Staff development and human resource offices have special contributions to offer within their areas of expertise. Other reform efforts may also be integrated with delivery of services to new teachers and contribute to the induction program.

Induction cannot become one more isolated program that rises and falls with funding levels and shifting priorities. It is that important that the induction program is viewed as an essential priority by top leadership.

COLLABORATION IN INDUCTION SERVICES

Most induction programs are complex and involve an array of persons and organizations. Sometimes districts collaborate to form an induction partnership, sharing talents, ideas, and resources among the schools they serve. Small school districts can benefit from working together to develop and implement a plan. Some collaborative groups are large and complex, involving many school districts and other organizations. Still others are coordinated through intermediate education agencies.

Very often, collaboration occurs within the school organization when other reform efforts become integrated with the induction program. For example, in a school adopting a new textbook series, all teachers (including the new teachers) are trained to use the series. Or perhaps a new program targeting low-performing students is initiated and the new teacher is involved in training for this effort. Some of these reform efforts have different funding sources and are managed by different leaders than those responsible for the induction program. However, a careful sharing of talent and resources among programs, where appropriate, can benefit all teachers, new and experienced alike. Those delivering induction program services need to be aware of the full range of activities that involve the new teacher so that the teacher can take part in all learning opportunities in an appropriate and timely way.

As pointed out earlier, other partners besides schools and school districts are sometimes involved. The local university may be involved in providing leadership, professional development, or even formal coursework. In some programs, other community partners have a role in the induction program because of the need to acquaint new teachers with their community environment. Research consultants may also be called upon to help with program evaluation activities.

Whenever multiple organizations and entities are involved in bringing the resources together, it is important that all parties work together and respect one another's roles and responsibilities. Huberman (1993) points out that sustained interaction and mutual influence are essential to successful collaborations. A formal written agreement can spell out those responsibilities so that there are not misunderstandings. Teachers need a planned, coherent, integrated program of induction rather than scattered attempts by many groups and individuals that are all trying to provide help and assistance.

SUPPORT OF SITE ADMINISTRATORS

The support of the site administrator is crucial to the success of the program at that particular school site. Site administrators need to understand and be supportive of the efforts made on behalf of the new teacher at their own sites. They should understand and support the goals of the induction program so that their own advice and counseling is consistent with the goals of the program and the vision of teaching that is being promoted. They need to support those who will assist and mentor the new teachers at their own sites.

Many site administrators see the support provided to new teachers by others as adjunct to their own responsibilities for assisting that teacher.

Although many site administrators often take on some responsibility for inducting the new teacher, their support role is somewhat different than that of the experienced teacher mentor. In actuality, the demands of the principalship may often preclude the kind of the intensive mentoring new teachers are able to receive from a colleague who has this as an assigned role. Teacher mentors fill the role of supportive guide and critical friend in listening, giving feedback, and providing guidance. Because the site administrator serves in an evaluative role, the new teacher is often reluctant to discuss areas of concern too openly. In fact, in many cases, the mentor will help to prepare the new teacher for the more formal evaluation that will be conducted by a site administrator.

Site administrators do play an important role in fostering a climate in which the dialogue between new teacher and mentor can occur most productively. They often give an initial orientation to the new teacher. They may be responsible for matching the mentor with the new teacher and providing time for them to work together. They may also plan or lead training sessions or meetings of mentors and protégés. They ensure that all site-level activities related to the induction program take place. They keep all teachers, new as well as experienced, focused on the vision of teaching that is subscribed to by the school, the district, and the state. They collect relevant data related to the implementation of the induction activities and participate in the evaluation of the program.

> One of our assistant principals is in charge of new teacher support. She runs the meetings for mentors and new teachers. She is really quite helpful. She has gotten to know us all very well.
>
> Second-year teacher

Many induction programs provide training for site administrators so that they become very familiar with the program and can be fully supportive. Site administrators who understand the role of the mentors and the professional development activities in which the teacher will engage can reinforce the messages that new teachers receive.

It is important that site administrators are supportive of and knowledgeable about the full range, purpose, and activities of the induction program. Site administrators who understand and support the induction activities are able to work more effectively with those who also providing support to ensure new teacher success.

UNIVERSITY LINKAGES

Induction takes place in the school where the teacher is employed, making induction the primary responsibility of the sponsoring school or district.

However, many induction programs have developed as partnerships among various organizations that have something to offer to the support of new teachers. In some programs, the university responsible for initial teacher preparation has become an active partner.

Universities have a stake in the performance of their graduates and gain information about their own programs by following their graduates into the field. The quality of preparation is reflected in the way their graduates perform in the classroom. Because state and national accrediting bodies now require that universities gather evidence about the success of their graduates, this interest has become even stronger than in the past.

While the university can benefit from knowledge about the progress of the new teacher, school districts can likewise benefit from knowledge about the new teacher's background. Induction planners should have an understanding of what new teachers bring in the way of preparation to their first teaching assignments. Teachers come to the classroom setting with certain understandings and perspectives that are to a large extent shaped by the preparation they received. If those assisting the new teacher are familiar with the preparation program, they will be able to build upon it, rather than simply repeat what has already been learned.

> Our interactions with university faculty have forced us to move beyond a survival mode to one of developing reflective practitioners who are able to analyze their own teaching and make thoughtful decisions.
>
> Induction program director

Each partner in a school-university partnership brings something different to the induction program. It is important for the partners to recognize and make use of the strengths that each brings.

School-based educators bring

- Familiarity with the problems facing new teachers
- An understanding of the setting and context in which the new teacher works
- Knowledge of the school culture
- An understanding of the curriculum the teacher is expect to teach
- An understanding about school and district expectations for the teacher

University-based educators bring

- Content expertise
- Expertise in pedagogy
- A previous helping relationship that is already established with the beginning teacher

- An understanding of beginning teaching and the needs of novice teachers
- Experience in staff development
- Research and evaluation experience

Those who are involved in school–university partnerships for induction programs emphasize the importance of regular communication and a respect for the culture, schedules, and work styles of the other organization. In the richest partnerships, the lines between preservice preparation and induction are becoming blurred. Educators in schools make contact early in the preparation cycle and contribute to the preservice preparation experience. University faculty members participate with mentors and their protégés in follow-up professional development activities and classroom observations. Sometimes the university student-teaching supervisor follows the new teacher into the new teacher's first teaching assignment.

The university linkages are even more crucial in the case of the alternate-route teacher who is enrolled in preparation courses while beginning to teach. This individual is both teacher and student and has both work and school responsibilities that need to be met. The induction program should help the alternate-route teacher deal with these multiple responsibilities rather than add unnecessarily to them.

Here is where collaboration becomes essential. School-based support providers and university faculty can work together to stage learning activities in a way that is beneficial for the teacher. Professional development and formal coursework can be modified and adapted so that it becomes complementary rather than repetitive.

Mentoring can help new teachers sort out and prioritize their multiple roles and responsibilities. The new teacher may have more than one person providing assistance—perhaps a university supervisor as well as a site-based mentor. The guidance these support providers give should be consistent and supportive of one another.

> We have new teacher meetings at our site. But they are covering stuff I already know. It is a waste of my time.
>
> First-year teacher

Well-designed alternate-route programs take advantage of and build upon the novice teacher's classroom experiences. They structure the learning experiences so that ideas and approaches can be tried out in that teacher's classroom and then discussed in class with others. Class sessions become more than theoretic discussions because the teacher is able to live out and test the learning each day in the classroom.

ATTENTION TO CONTEXT

Teachers are socialized into a profession during the induction period, but they experience their professional responsibilities, their successes, and their challenges in a particular context. Some important aspects of this context are the working conditions and the culture of the school and community.

Teachers' perceptions are shaped by a variety of factors related to their own work location. The following contextual characteristics all play a role in shaping workplace conditions for teachers:

- School type
- Class size
- Workload
- Availability of resources
- Student characteristics
- School climate
- Collegial relations
- Parental involvement

Schools differ in important ways across these dimensions that help to make up the context that impact teachers and their work. Each of these factors is examined here in light of the implications for beginning teachers.

School type. Teachers may begin the work in a public or private school. They may work in an urban, rural, or suburban community. They may work at the elementary, middle, or high school level in a school that is small, medium, or large in size. Teachers need to know and understand the type of school and community in which they are working. It may be unlike the type of school in which they themselves were schooled, or where they did their student teaching.

A teacher schooled primarily in small, selective private schools in a suburban area may find herself working in a large, urban school setting. A middle school teacher may have been placed at that site but would have preferred a high school placement. A teacher may not have desired a teaching position in the central city, but took the position because that was where jobs were readily available or because there was a financial incentive to do so. A teacher working in an affluent suburb may not be able to afford to live near his work setting and may have to commute a long distance to get to work. In each case, the context will play a role in shaping the teacher's perceptions and performance.

Teachers need to develop an understanding of and appreciation for the context in which they find themselves. They also need to understand the developmental characteristics of the students at their particular level so they know what to expect of students and how to guide their learning.

Each type of school brings its own challenges for the beginning teacher. In small schools, for example, a new teacher may be the only person teaching at a particular grade level, or in a particular subject area, and will not be able to rely on experienced colleague on site who is teaching in the same area. Large schools are often too impersonal to create an effective support program in which the entire school embraces the induction program. Urban schools often serve a large number of impoverished students, many of whom are English-language learners. In suburban schools, parents typically have extremely high expectations of their schools and can place extraordinary pressure on both students and teachers.

Schools and their communities often have deep and rich traditions that help to define them. New teachers will be more effective if they come to understand those communities and their traditions. They need to understand the special characteristics and features that impact student learning in their communities.

Class size. A number of state and federal reform efforts in recent years have focused on reducing class size in targeted grades (usually the early elementary) and in specific key subject areas (such as English) where smaller classes have are considered particularly desirable in fostering student learning. As popular as this move has been with teachers and parents, the research related to the connections between class size and student achievement has been mixed (Biddle & Berliner, 2002). However, teachers (as well as parents) generally prefer to have smaller classes and believe that smaller classes enables them to give each child more individual attention. New teachers feel particularly challenged when they are given large classes and not enough assistance. Some induction programs are designed to support the new teacher by assigning smaller class sizes than would be normal or by providing paraprofessionals to assist the new teachers. Unusually large classes add to the challenges for new teachers and should be avoided.

Workload. A recent national study found that the average amount of time the average teacher spends on all teaching activities (i.e., preparing for class, teaching, grading student work, filling out reports) is approximately 45.5 hours per week (Henke, Choy, Chen, Geis, Alt, & Broughman, 1997). However, new teachers often spend considerably more time than that because they have not developed a collection of lesson plans, ideas, and materials to rely upon, nor have they developed strategies for efficiently and effectively evaluating student work, completing reports, and attending to the many other outside-of-class responsibilities.

The size of the class can have an impact on the teacher's workload, as can some other factors related to the teacher's work assignment. Some schools have developed policies related to new teacher assignment that recognize their novice status. Many avoid putting new teachers in multigrade classes at the elementary level, or protect the secondary teacher from an unusually large number of different preparations. It is also helpful for new teachers to have a single, assigned classroom for the entire day, rather than requiring that they travel from classroom to classroom between periods.

Availability of resources. Teachers need an ample supply of books, teaching materials, and other resources to do their work. Yet we know that classrooms are not equally well equipped and that teachers often end up having to purchase many materials from their own funds. New teachers are especially ill-equipped in this regard. Many induction programs provide some start-up funds for new teachers to defray some of these expenses and to enable teachers to purchase appropriate and useful classroom materials. Mentors can assist new teachers by sharing materials and resources, and by helping teachers make a good selection of resources. They can also provide advice about sources of materials and about making good selections.

Resource issues can be a key source of frustration to the new teacher. The research demonstrates a perceived difference among teachers regarding the adequacy of resources depending on where they work. The extent to which teachers report having adequate teaching resources varies by school sector, size, and the income level of students. Again, our urban schools are disadvantaged in this regard. Teachers in larger schools with more low-income students typically report less access to adequate materials (Henke et al., 1997).

Resource allocations help to determine the level and intensity of support provided for induction activities. Resources need to be made available to provide release time for new teachers and their mentors to work together, in and out of the classroom. Resources are also needed to fund appropriate professional development activities. In this current period of declining resources, it is important to maintain the level of support that has been characteristic of our best, more richly funded induction programs that have demonstrated strong success.

Student characteristics. Teachers can be most effective in meeting students' learning needs if they know the backgrounds and characteristics of their students. What is their socioeconomic level? How have they performed in the past? What is their first language? What are their cultural traditions and beliefs? What is their family status? What are their preferred learning styles? What are the particular challenges to learning that they face?

Because teaching assignments are most often made on the basis of seniority, the new teacher is often assigned a group of students that may be particularly challenging to manage and teach, even for the more experienced, expert teacher.

Policies and practices related to teaching assignments are often subject to collective bargaining agreements. Many factors are involved, including the long-standing practice of rewarding those with seniority with first choice of teaching assignments. However, some districts have been able to modify their policies to give attention to the careful assignment of novices so that they do not get the most difficult assignments. Where there is local discretion, assignment of new teachers should receive high priority for special attention.

When the new teacher has a particularly challenging class because of size or student characteristics, that teacher may need extra assistance. This could come in the form of assistance from a paraprofessional, parent volunteers, or more intensive mentoring.

School climate. Another aspect of the context for beginning teaching is the climate or culture of the individual school. Each school develops a culture of its own based on the beliefs, attitudes, and practices of the people who work there, as well as the community expectations for the school. Feiman-Nemser and Floden (1986) define the teaching culture as "embodied in the work-related beliefs and knowledge teachers share—beliefs about acting in appropriate ways on the job and rewarding aspects of teaching, and knowledge that enables teachers to do their work" (p. 508).

New teachers are shaped by the culture of the school in which they work and often begin to take on the beliefs and practices of their colleagues, even if it is at odds with what they have learned. As Page (1987) states: "the culture of a school both shapes teachers' understanding of their mode of operation and of their students and is grounded in faculty members' shared decisions" (p. 90).

Much work has focused on the detrimental effects of low teacher expectations for students that often predominates the culture of urban schools. For example, Page (1987) found dramatic differences in teacher expectations for students depending on the social class of the students served. The culture of the school was linked to the larger social order and shared perceptions of capabilities of students and expectations of parents. In other words, "the culture is reflected and recreated in the classroom as teachers provide the school's version of a curriculum appropriate for students of a particular social class" (p. 90).

Inducting teachers into this type of culture is counterproductive. Teachers need other, more positive and empowering support systems to shape their thinking and the enactment of their own teaching beliefs and practices. Induction programs are attempting to not only provide better role models, but also set about actually changing the culture of the school as a workplace.

Tushnet et al. (2002) point out that successful induction programs are found in schools where the entire school views the induction of new teachers as a collective responsibility. Their research indicates that the principal plays a crucial role in creating a school climate that is conducive to supporting new teachers.

Other attributes of the school climate relate to the characteristics of the physical environment and location in which one works. Old, deteriorating buildings that are in disrepair are hardly conducive to retention of highly qualified and motivated teachers that may have other options. Likewise, a neighborhood in a high crime area may discourage teachers from remaining.

Again, our deteriorating urban schools are at a disadvantage in this regard. A recent national survey reports that a large majority of teachers and principals report their schools to be clean, safe, and quiet, and that they have enough classrooms. However, teachers in urban schools are less likely than those in suburban or rural schools to be working in a clean and orderly environment. Teachers with higher percentage of low-income students are less likely than teachers who serve a wealthier population to describe their schools as clean, safe, and not too noisy for students to concentrate (Metropolitan Life Insurance Company, 2001).

> The environment is challenging. If there were more students who wanted to succeed, they could motivate others. They have low expectations of each other.
>
> First-year urban teacher

Induction programs cannot solve these larger problems. In fact, if these conditions continue to exist, teachers will continue to leave urban schools in large numbers. Addressing these conditions will help to establish a better working environment for new teachers, but will also benefit all teachers and students. This takes a broader commitment on the part of policy makers and educational leaders at all levels to revitalize and refurbish schools in our blighted urban areas.

Collegial relationships. Teaching has traditionally been a very isolating profession, one in which teachers close their classroom doors and seldom interact with other adults. Such professional isolation promotes the old "sink-or-swim" approach, and teachers fail to learn and benefit from conversations with other professionals. Through our induction programs, we have begun to value and appreciate the advantage of viewing teaching as a more collaborative endeavor, and teachers are learning from each other.

This collegiality has always existed at some schools, in some locations, and among some teachers within particular schools. However, we have only recently begun to think about intentionally designing strategies and providing structured opportunities that might foster and develop more collegial relations among teachers. New teacher induction programs find a variety of ways to nurture and foster collegial conversation.

Parental involvement. It is generally thought that strong parental involvement is conducive to providing a better learning experience for students. The degree and level of parental support varies by school, community, and location. In one national study, 28% of teachers reported that lack of parental support was a serious problem in their schools (Henke et al., 1997). New teachers are especially challenged by their role in working with parents, and are uncertain about how to gain parental support. When the climate at a school is unwelcoming to parents, or when the school does not actively seek to involve parents, the new teacher often gives in to the prevailing notion that the parents just don't care or are not supportive of their work.

> Parents are too busy working just to keep the family going. They don't know what to do with their children; they have poor parenting skills. They need education themselves—parenting classes. They don't come in to school. We have a parenting center and everything. I'm not quite sure how that works, however.
>
> First-year teacher

New teachers need to be encouraged to work with parents as partners in fostering the child's learning, but need to learn to do so in a culture and environment that encourages that partnership. If the school feels uninviting and unwelcoming to parents, it will be hard for an individual new teacher to change that perception.

Workplace conditions are important in establishing the context for beginning teaching. These conditions (school type, class size, workload, availability of resources, student characteristics, school climate, collegial relations, and parental involvement) should all be considered and attended to in developing induction policies and programs that are successful in supporting and furthering the development of new teachers. New teachers (and all teachers) will develop most positive attitudes and be more productive and effective if the appropriate workplace conditions support and encourage them in their work.

Workplace conditions may discourage teachers from choosing or remaining in the schools that serve our poorest children. Special attention needs to be paid to the working conditions in schools that serve low-income students if we want to attract and retain well-qualified teachers in these settings. Teachers and students alike will benefit if we address these conditions in more proactive ways than we have in the past.

EXPERIENCED TEACHERS AS SUPPORT PROVIDERS

The idea of the more experienced teachers assisting novices is not new. What is relatively new is the systematic approach to organizing, training, and providing a structure within an induction program for that to occur.

Mentoring is at the heart of most new teacher induction programs. Many argue that the mentoring relationship is one that cannot be structured or "forced" among colleagues but should be left to occur naturally. That is not the position held by those who are intentional about designing induction programs for all new teachers. The benefits of mentoring are too important to assume that it will occur naturally, without a structure and a plan to make it happen for all new teachers.

While the mentoring relationship is one that is a highly personal one, if care is taken in selecting, arranging matches, training, and preparing mentors, the likelihood of success is high that the mentoring relationship can be developed and nurtured.

The roles and responsibilities of mentors need to be made clear from the outset. It is best to spend some time thinking about what mentors will do and how they will perform their work. How and when will they be expected to work with new teachers? Will they observe in teachers' classrooms? Will they conduct demonstration lessons? Will they meet on a regular basis? Will they arrange for other professional development? Will they attend meetings with new teachers? How often will a mentor meet individually with the new teacher? These expectations should be specified in writing and communicated to all program participants.

Mentors should be selected carefully for their ability to perform the roles that have been carefully specified. Many programs develop specific criteria to be used in the selection process, recognizing that not all teachers are suited for this role.

Those who serve as mentors need to be prepared for their unique roles. Most induction programs include a formal training experience for mentors and ongoing discussions among mentors about their work with new teachers. Mentors realize that they need to learn about how to be effective in providing the appropriate guidance, support, and feedback to new teachers. They understand how to work with adult learners, solve problems, and resolve conflicts. They seek not to provide all the answers to a new teacher, but are able to guide the teacher in self-discovery, reflection, and critical examination of teaching practices and learning results.

Much has been learned about the mentoring role in induction programs as a result of research conducted in the past several decades. A fuller discussion of mentoring relationships, strategies, and approaches is found in Chapter 4.

TIME TO WORK TOGETHER

The nature of a mentoring relationship in an induction program calls for a planned, structured time for teachers to work together. Mentors are able to observe teachers in their classrooms, model demonstration lessons, provide feedback, and discuss teaching practices and areas of concern with the new teachers.

Many induction program sponsors find that the most effective approach is to release classroom teachers from all of their own classroom duties and to assign them a number of new teachers to work with on a regular, full-time basis. One of the longest running induction programs in California (Moir, Gless, & Baron, 1999) uses this model, which is described as follows:

> At the center of our work are the partnerships that form between the beginning teachers and the new-teacher advisors, exemplary teachers on loan from participating districts for two or three years. Matched with beginning teachers according to grade level and subject matter expertise, each advisor mentors 14 first- and second-year teachers. (p. 108)

We have found that supporting new teachers is complex and demanding work and that it involves learning skills other than those most classroom teachers possess. Providing this support becomes even harder when advisors must simultaneously focus on the needs of students in their own classrooms. Supporting new teachers after the school day ends makes it difficult to understand a new teacher's classroom circumstances, his or her level of practice, and the students' needs.

Moir et al. (1999, p. 112)

These program sponsors find that the quality of this intensive mentoring relationship and the day-to-day guidance that the experience veterans can provide under the full-time release model is a key ingredient in their program.

Another model often found is the partial release of mentors from their own classroom assignments. For example, a mentor may be released one day or one-half day per week to work with a limited number of new teachers. This model is most effective when the mentor is supporting novices at their own site and can supplement the planned time with informal conversations between formal meetings.

Finally, there are induction programs where there are not sufficient funds to release classroom teachers from their regular teaching duties. Mentoring in these programs usually takes place after school, during lunch periods, planning periods, or on evenings or weekends. Because time to work together is an important ingredient in effective induction programs, it is much more difficult to ensure adequate support with this model.

The key to rich, productive meetings of new teachers and their mentors are that they occur on a regular and frequent basis, perhaps as often as once a week. In addition, the mentor needs to get into the new teachers classroom and actually observe the new teacher in action in order to provide effective support and feedback.

> We met once a week on Wednesdays. But my mentor is right next door so if I had questions I could always ask. She didn't mind answering all my questions.
>
> Second-year teacher

The regular, ongoing meetings and observations are supplemented with informal discussion and interaction that may occur more informally during and after the school day. These conversations can occur in the hallways, lunchroom, and in the teachers' lounge. Increasingly, new teachers and their mentors are using e-mail to keep in touch with one another or joining the growing number of online discussion groups.

PROFESSIONAL DEVELOPMENT FOR NEW TEACHERS

In addition to mentoring, new-teacher support often includes a variety of professional development opportunities that are designed specifically for new teachers. These might include meetings, workshops, training, or additional university classes. The focus of these activities is to help expand the teacher's knowledge, acquaint teachers with specific curricula or district practices, expose them new ideas and strategies, and provide a context for further learning. In some cases, new teachers find it valuable to participate in meetings with other new teachers to share ideas and experiences, and learn from one another.

Professional development for new teachers is not designed to "reteach" what was already learned in the preparation program, but is an extension and application of that prior learning to the teacher's own classroom. It provides an opportunity for bringing new teachers together in groups to discuss their progress, share challenges, and learn from each other.

Care needs to be taken in planning group meetings and professional development activities so that they are perceived as relevant, challenging, and of interest to the new teacher. Professional development for teachers has not always been well received or valued by teachers.

Professional development should be based on our best knowledge of the principles adult learning (see Exhibit 3.2) and should engage teachers in problem solving and reflection. Teachers should be viewed as highly competent and motivated individuals who are always willing to learn more and improve. They come with a knowledge base, skills, and beliefs. They are presented with ideas to think about, expand upon, and apply in

Exhibit 3.2 Principles of Adult Learning

1. Adults need to know why they need to learn something before undertaking it.

2. Adults are self-directed learners.

3. Experience is the richest resource for adult learning.

4. Adults become ready to learn when they are convinced they need to know something in order to cope with their life situation.

5. Adults are life-centered in their orientation to learning. They learn new knowledge, understanding, skills, values, and attitudes most effectively when presented in the context of application to real-life situations.

6. While adults are subject to some external motivators, the most potent motivators are internal pressures.

Knowles, Holton, and Swanson (1998)

their own way in their own classrooms rather than a plan that needs to be followed like a recipe. They work together to plan and implement these ideas and practices, in their own settings, with their own students. And, finally, the professional development should be based on teachers' own needs rather than on dictated mandates.

There are certain instances when a whole-group approach is the most effective and efficient starting point for new teachers, when there are things that induction program planners can be sure that will benefit all new teachers. One such instance is the initial orientation to the district. Many districts begin with an intensive group orientation program for all new teachers. This orientation is intended to acquaint the new teacher with the school and community, district policies and practices, and, often, current reform efforts. Some last several days and some may extend a full week. Exhibit 3.3 is an example schedule for one initial orientation program.

Other opportunities for teachers to meet regularly as a group can also be effective. Some programs offer regular new-teacher meetings by grade level or by subject area. This allows teachers the opportunity to meet with others who share their curriculum and grade-level issues and concerns. Teachers find these meetings most helpful if their issues and concerns are the focus of the discussion.

Some professional development plans offer a menu of selections for the new teacher, and the choice of what to attend is made by new teachers in collaboration with their mentors. The most effective professional development is geared to individual needs of the new teacher and engages the teacher in critical reflection on their own work. Because of the wide variation the knowledge and skills teachers bring to their first position and differing levels of preparation, teachers' needs vary according to their circumstances.

New teachers often find that required workshops interfere with their own preparation and planning time, sometimes adding to their stresses

Exhibit 3.3 Sample Orientation Schedule

Time	Day One	Day Two	Day Three
8:00–9:00	Opening Session • Welcome • Orientation overview • BTSA induction program	Opening Session • Welcome • Program overview • Child abuse reporting	Opening Session • Welcome • Section 504 of the Rehabilitation Act • IEP presentation
9:00–9:15	Break	Break	Break
9:15–12:15	Rotations • Parent involvement • Equity for all students • Hot tips for teachers: strategies for increasing student engagement • Instructional media center tour	Rotations • Parent involvement • Equity for all students • Hot tips for teachers: strategies for increasing student engagement • Instructional media center tour	Rotations • Parent involvement • Equity for all students • Hot tips for teachers: strategies for increasing student engagement • Instructional media center tour
12:15–1:00	Lunch	Lunch	Lunch
1:00–4:00	Content sessions • Math • Science • Social Studies • World Languages • Special Education • Physical Education • Visual and Performing Arts • Technology • Other	Content sessions • Math • Science • Social Studies • World Languages • Special Education • Physical Education • Visual and Performing Arts • Technology • Other	Content sessions • Math • Science • Social Studies • World Languages • Special Education • Physical Education • Visual and Performing Arts • Technology • Other

Source: San Diego City Schools (2003).

during the first year. This is particularly so for the alternate route teacher, who is probably taking classes at night to obtain a full credential. Additional meetings or workshops, unless considered highly valuable, are often seen as a detracting from their preparation time. Professional development for the new teacher should be planned carefully and evaluated for its ability to meet the new teacher's needs.

Exhibit 3.4 Effective Professional Development

Effective professional development:

1) Is driven fundamentally by analyses of the differences between (a) goals and standards for student learning and (b) student performance.

2) Involves learners (such as teachers) in the identification of their learning needs and, when possible, the development of the learning opportunity and/or the process to be used.

3) Is primarily school based and integral to school operations.

4) Provides learning opportunities that relate to individual needs but for the most part are organized around collective problem solving.

5) Is continuous and ongoing, involving follow-up and support for further learning, including support from sources external to the school.

6) Incorporates evaluation of multiple sources of information on outcomes for student and processes involved in implementing the lessons learned through professional development.

7) Provides opportunities to develop a theoretical understanding of the knowledge and skills to be learned.

8) Is integrated with a comprehensive change process that deals with the full range of impediments to and facilitators of student learning.

Hawley and Valli (1999, p. 138)

FOLLOW-UP BY EXPERIENCED EDUCATORS

We have learned a great deal about what constitutes an effective professional development for teachers (see Exhibit 3.4). Rarely do single, isolated workshops provide the desired results if we want teachers to take new knowledge and apply it in classrooms. Joyce and Showers (2002) indicate that the most successful outcomes can be achieved through a combination of providing: information, theory, demonstration and practice, feedback, and coaching in the new ideas or teaching strategies. Professional development deemed useful incorporates all of these strategies and is targeted to the very specific needs of new teachers.

Follow-up occurs as teachers practice their new skills and reflect on that practice with others. They ask questions of the mentor and their peers and have an opportunity to observe other teachers who demonstrate the practices being addressed. They consult with others who can guide and provide advice about specific needs. They work together to problem-solve and to try out new ideas.

The mentor who supports the new teacher is in a strong position to provide this coaching and feedback; or perhaps, in specialized areas, another coach will be trained to help provide feedback and follow up on a specific strategy, curriculum, or approach.

FEEDBACK TO BEGINNING TEACHERS

Developing teachers want feedback about how they are doing. However, they need feedback that is specific to their own needs and focused on their own readiness. In some cases, teachers self-identify their needs and are able to ask for help. For example, they may say they need help with planning or classroom management. However, in most cases, it is difficult for new teachers to identify what specific help they may need, or why they have difficulty with planning or classroom management.

Skilled mentors are able to help new teacher identify those more subtle needs—and are able to help the teacher reflect on strategies to strengthen teaching and improve student learning. There are able help new teachers broaden their repertoire of skills and strategies, and to try new approaches. The induction program needs to prepare mentors to engage in this deep, rich reflection on practice with the new teachers.

This reflection on practice is enriched by assessments of the new teacher's knowledge and skills. Many early (and some current) induction programs avoided the use of any kind of assessment of teacher performance, fearing that the judgmental nature of assessments would interfere with the mentoring relationship. In fact, in many programs, assessments do perform a gatekeeping function, helping to discern whether or not to award the teacher a professional license.

However, assessments can serve a much broader purpose. Assessments can help to highlight areas of strength and weakness for the teacher and can be used in a formative sense to shape the mentoring professional development of the new teacher. There are assessment tools and approaches that can help provide that deeper and richer look at teaching practice. Examples of these assessment tools and their application to induction programs are described in Chapter 7.

> What is the biggest help to me are the classroom observations. I really like it when people come to observe. They have given me so much good feedback. I really find it helpful.
>
> First-year teacher

EVALUATION OF THE PROGRAM

Effective induction practices can lead to improved practice for new teachers and improved learning for students. We know that because others have evaluated and documented their work in teacher induction.

However, not all programs are equally effective in achieving the desired ends. Programs are sometimes implemented in a very uneven way across districts or school sites. Every induction program should continue to be evaluated so that the program planners and participants know what is most effective.

Most programs evaluate each element of the program. Are the professional development activities designed for teachers perceived as helpful? Are teachers attending those workshops? If there is a menu of activities from which to select, what professional development activities are selected and why are they selected? How are these sessions followed up in the classroom? What did teachers learn? Are teaching practices changed as a result of this learning? Is the mentoring occurring on a regular basis? Are mentors perceived as offering helpful guidance? How often do teachers and their mentors meet? Are the matches successful? If not, why not? Which school sites seem to be most effective in implementing the program and why? What is the role of the site administrator in supporting the program? How is this support realized?

If a program is clear about its purpose and goals, the evaluation can be designed to gather information about how well the program is achieving those goals. Are teachers being retained in higher numbers? Are they more satisfied with their work? Are they more successful in the classroom? Are they engaging in practices consistent with the standards we have set for them? Are their students more successful?

These are some of the important evaluation questions that need to be central to how we examine our induction programs and activities. Exhibit 3.5 reviews the key elements of effective induction programs and suggests evaluation questions that might help assess each component. Programs need to examine their practices and their outcomes on a regular basis and then adjust programs on the basis of their findings.

IMPLICATIONS FOR PRACTICE

This chapter has summarized the characteristics of effective induction programs. Effective induction programs

1. Are clear about the purpose and intended outcomes of the program.

2. Give sufficient attention to leadership and administration of the program.

3. Foster collaboration among organizations, groups, and individuals involved in providing induction services.

4. Ensure support of site administrators who are well informed about the purpose and goals of the program.

5. Are knowledgeable about and include linkages with the university preparation program that prepare the teacher for practice.

Exhibit 3.5 Evaluation Questions for Induction Programs

Program Features	Evaluation Questions
Purpose and goals	Are the purposes and goals clear to all participants? Are program plans aligned with the goals?
Intended outcomes	How well and how consistently are the intended outcomes (i.e., retention, teacher satisfaction, improved teacher and student performance) being met?
Leadership and administration	What are the qualifications of those selected for leadership roles? What are the perceived and actual roles of the leadership team? How are resources allocated?
Collaboration	What are the collaborative arrangements? How are the collaborations implemented? What is the commitment level of the partners? What roles do they play? What makes the collaborations successful or not successful?
Support of site administrators	How are site administrators oriented to their roles? To what extent do they understand and accept their responsibilities? What roles do they actually play? How do program participants perceive the participation of site administrators?
Linkages with university preparation	What is the relationship of preservice learning and professional development in induction? How and to what extent are these linkages made?
New-teacher assignment	How are new-teacher assignments made? How are new teachers made aware of the expectations of their specific assignments?
Context	How do new teachers come to understand the contexts in which they work? What aspects of the context contribute to new-teacher satisfaction or dissatisfaction?
Mentoring	Who is selected as mentors and how are they selected and trained? How do they evaluate their own training and follow up activities? How do they work with new teachers? What ongoing support is provided to mentors? How do new teachers perceive the effectiveness of the mentors?
Provision of scheduled, structured time	How much time is spent working together and what takes place during that time? How helpful is it perceived to be by the new teachers? What assistance is perceived to be most helpful or least helpful?
Professional development	How are professional development activities geared to stages of readiness? How do new teachers rate each of the activities? What training is sought and why?
Individual follow-up	What follow up is provided and how is it provided? How does the training and follow up impact classroom practice?
Feedback to beginning teachers	How is teacher performance assessed? What feedback is provided? How is that feedback used to inform conversations with new teachers? How does teacher performance change as a result of receiving feedback?
Evaluation	Are all important aspects of the program evaluated? How are evaluation findings used to shape the program?

6. Give attention to the context in which new teachers are assigned to work and their specific teaching assignments.

7. Include the involvement of experienced teacher mentors who are carefully selected and trained to effectively guide and assist new teachers.

8. Provide scheduled, structured time for experienced and beginning teachers to work together.

9. Include professional development for new teachers—training that is related to their immediate needs and their current stage of professional development.

10. Provide for individual follow-up by experienced educators so that new teachers learn to use new skills effectively in their classrooms.

11. Give feedback to beginning teachers about their progress in meeting professional goals and expectations.

12. Evaluate the program and its impact on new teachers and their students.

FOR FURTHER READING

Portner, H. (2001). *Training mentors is not enough: Everything else schools and districts need to do.* Thousand Oaks, CA: Corwin.
The author points out that a mentoring program is part of a broader macrosystem in an expanded view of the mentoring process. This book's purpose is to help the reader (a) obtain a broad-based commitment from, and participation of, key individuals and groups; (b) understand and work within the larger environment in which a mentoring program operates; (c) form a mentoring committee and develop its capacity to make decisions effectively; and (d) support the program with pragmatic and effective policies, procedures, and resources. The book is a resource for planning, managing, and evaluating mentoring programs.

Richin, R., Banyon, R., Stein, R. P., & Banyon, F. (2003). *Induction: Connecting teacher recruitment to retention.* Thousand Oaks, CA: Corwin.
This book provides readers with the effective practices for attracting and keeping educators by using five building blocks to construct a three-year practical plan to recruit and retain staff. It is organized to respond to the developmental stages of the teacher's career and includes

- Preparing: recognizing your induction needs, developing your mission statement, establishing policy, and setting your induction goals.
- Staffing: recruiting, interviewing, and hiring.
- Orienting—year one: conducting professional development; mentoring and collaborating; and supervising, observing, and evaluating.
- Connecting—years two and three: continuing professional development as well as supervising, observing, and evaluating; granting tenure/permanence.

- Keeping/retaining: sustaining the connection, developing career long learners, and renewing and reorienting.

Scherer, M. (Ed.). (1999). *A better beginning: Supporting and mentoring new teachers.* Alexandria, VA: Association for Supervision and Curriculum Development.
This rich collection of articles, written by a variety of authors, covers the following topics:
- What do new teachers need?
- Creating an induction program
- Making mentoring meaningful
- Planning comprehensive teacher support
- Improving instruction and communication
- Listening to teachers

Sweeny, B. W. (2001). *Leading the teacher induction and mentoring program.* Arlington Heights, IL: Skylight Training and Publishing.
This book takes school leaders through the process of creating and sustaining an induction and mentoring program, challenging the reader to think beyond initial, short-term goals to a wider, long-term vision. It provides guidance on telementoring in the cyberage and advice to ensure development of highly effective practices that will improve teaching and student learning.

Villani, S. (2001). *Mentoring programs for new teachers: Models of induction and support.* Thousand Oaks, CA: Corwin.
The value of mentoring programs for teacher training and retention is widely recognized. This author offers a number of ways in which schools, teacher associations, institutions of higher education, state agencies, and other induction sponsors can support teachers with the right mentoring and induction program at the right time. It covers the design, as well as delivery, of programs. Topics include
- Inducting new teachers.
- Continuing program design.
- Models of mentoring.
- District-funded programs.
- Peer assistance and review programs.
- State-funded programs.
- Grant- and alternative-funded programs.

4

Mentoring Strategies and Best Practices

Mentoring plays an important role in most teacher induction programs. Mentors are most effective if they are carefully selected, prepared for their responsibilities, supported in their work, and evaluated on a regular basis. New teachers need mentoring that is appropriate to their needs. They should be mentored toward a defined vision of effective teaching. This chapter focuses on mentoring strategies and approaches that have been particularly successful in a variety of school contexts.

THE ROLE OF MENTORING IN INDUCTION

Mentoring is often an important ingredient in an induction program. New teachers indicate that assistance and guidance by a more experienced colleague plays a crucial role in helping them succeed. Mentors listen, give advice, encourage, demonstrate practices, and brainstorm with novice teachers on a wide variety of issues. Mentors are available when new teachers simply feel overwhelmed and need someone to listen. They help teachers learn how to work with students, interact with parents, work with their colleagues, and respond to the demands of administrators. They work through general and specific problems with the new teachers. They keep new teachers focused on student learning and help guide them to more effective practice.

> My mentor is the head of my department. She has all these lessons and so many ideas. I go to her all the time.
>
> Second-year teacher

Mentoring can occur naturally, without a planned program. It occurs when the novice teacher learns to rely on the teacher next door, who will listen, give practical tips to the new teacher, and share lesson plans and materials. However, this does not always happen automatically.

Little (1990) reminds us that teaching has traditionally been a very isolating profession and that "norms of collegiality" in a school setting are, in reality, quite rare. The nature of the work of teaching makes conversations among professionals difficult. Teachers spend most of their workday in their own classroom with their own students. They seldom work together or have opportunities to observe one another. Conversations among teachers about their work are confined to breaks and lunchtime, and perhaps a planning period when they often have other priorities to attend to such as getting caught up on paperwork, phone calls to parents, and other duties.

Often, the informal conversations among teachers are brief and disjointed, and sometimes more negative than helpful. Teachers' lounges are notorious for being places where teachers vent their complaints about students, other teachers, administrators, and parents. New teachers can be too easily influenced by the negative picture that is too often conveyed.

Some teachers report that their colleagues seem to be absorbed by their own responsibilities and do not want to share ideas, materials, and other resources. Some, in fact, are quite proprietary, and are unwilling to share what they have spent a career developing and refining.

> A lot of teachers are into their own work. I'm never comfortable approaching them; they seem too busy.
>
> First-year teacher

Because of the challenges and threats to this natural collegiality among teachers, mentoring is organized and structured in the induction program.

THE CONCEPT OF MENTORING

The word "mentor" comes from the classic tale of the *Odyssey* (Dimock, 1989) in which Odysseus entrusted the care, nurturing, and upbringing of his son, Telemachus, to his old and trusted friend, Mentor. Mentor encourages, supports, and guides Telemachus as he finds his way in life and develops his adult identity. Thus the term mentor has become associated with the role of the more experienced person who guides and supports the protégé.

Mentors can be found in our personal and professional lives. Mentors are usually older or more experienced colleagues who provide support to and watch over the progress of younger, or less experienced, individuals. Mentors listen, advise, promote, nurture, suggest, guide, respond, suggest, encourage, and seek to develop the skills and abilities of their protégés. They are role models for novices, living and practicing what they advocate.

> When I work with a new teacher, I always remember the challenges of my own first year.
>
> Mentor teacher

It is only in the last two decades that mentoring has gradually found a more formal role in the teacher-development continuum. During this time, we have learned much about the potential and practice of mentoring in the educational context. Mentoring has become a powerful tool and resource in helping to retain and acculturate teachers to their roles and to the profession.

Many terms have been used to describe this unique role that is played by the more experienced teacher such as mentor, critical friend, buddy, coach, teacher-advisor, consultant, teammate, and support provider. Although it may be argued that each of these terms conveys a slightly different kind of relationship between novice and experienced teacher, each term does acknowledge that teachers have the responsibility to assist one another as they enhance their teaching skills and develop their own professional practice.

In this book, the term "mentor" is used to designate that guiding role, no matter what it is named by the individual program sponsor.

> *Mentoring: Professional practice that occurs in the context of teaching whenever an experienced teacher supports, challenges, and guides novice teachers in their teaching practice.*
>
> **Odell and Huling (2000, p. xv)**

THE BENEFITS OF MENTORING

The research in California demonstrated the benefits of effective mentoring for teachers and their students. When compared with other new teachers who do not have access to mentoring, beginning teachers who are well-mentored more consistently (a) use instructional practices that improve student achievement; (b) use more complex, challenging instructional activities that enabled students to learn advanced thinking skills and cooperative work habits; (c) engage in long-term planning of curriculum and instruction, ensuring that students are taught the entire set of skills and knowledge to be learned during the year; (d) motivate diverse students to engage in productive learning activities; and (e) give the same complex, challenging assignments to classes of diverse pupils as they do to classes that were ethnically and culturally homogeneous (Bartell, 1995).

Because mentoring is too important to leave to chance, most induction programs structure the mentoring experience and establish expectations and guidelines for implementation. Mentors are assigned to new teachers and work them on a regular basis. This provides a structure and a plan for bringing the knowledge and expertise of the more experienced educator to the new teacher and helps to break down the barriers and isolation among teachers in schools.

In the most successful programs, mentors understand and represent a vision of teaching that is consistent with an explicit vision of teaching. They know how to describe, model, assess, and give feedback to new teachers about achieving that vision.

In the many early induction programs, the purpose of mentoring was seen primarily as helping the novice survive and begin to develop basic teaching skills. It was thought that mentoring would help to reduce early "burnout" and keep more novices in the profession. While teacher retention is still a goal of many mentoring and induction programs, we have realized that mentoring can accomplish much more. It can help to shape teaching practice and help teachers become competent and highly successful earlier in their careers.

> I have gotten so much help. Immediately I was assigned a great mentor. In addition to that, the math department chair was doing the National Boards and he was another mentor to me. So I had two. Actually, any experienced teacher here that you ask for help will give it.
>
> Third-year teacher

Some maintain that a structured mentoring program with assigned mentors cannot duplicate the natural relationship that is the basis of the more informal mentoring that emerges naturally between colleagues. However, we cannot assume that every new teacher will automatically receive needed help without structured provisions and guidelines for making that help available. Most do not receive this kind of help. Structuring the mentoring relationship in a careful, thoughtful way is necessary to make this a good relationship and to ensure that mentoring will actually occur.

MENTORING TOWARD A VISION

Mentoring is not a panacea. As Feiman-Nemser (1996) points out in her review of the literature on mentoring, "The education community understands that mentors have a positive effect on teacher retention, but that leaves open the question of what mentors should do, what they actually do, and what novices learn as a result" (p. 1).

More contemporary views of mentoring reflect the new accountability environment in which we live and work. Because effecting mentoring can have such positive outcomes, we develop programs to help give all new teachers access to the assistance of a more experienced colleague and we develop a structure to ensure that it will occur. A key piece of that structure is a well-defined vision of teaching and learning that becomes a focus of the mentoring experience itself. Mentors and novices work toward a set of expectations about what teachers ought to know and be able to do, and what good teaching looks like in actual practice. The vision suggested here is one of reflective practice. That vision is discussed more extensively in Chapter 6.

This vision gives focus and direction to mentoring. Mentors themselves need to understand and embrace this vision so that they able to help and guide new teachers. Mentors help teachers grow and learn so that they are able to realize and enact that vision in their own classrooms.

SELECTION OF MENTORS

It is important to give attention to the careful selection of mentors who will guide new teachers. Not every good teacher will necessarily be an effective mentor to other teachers. Working with adults and guiding their learning takes different skills than working with young persons. However, it is essential that mentors be strong teachers if they are to be role models for other teachers and help novices become better teachers. Mentors need to be able to enact that vision of excellent teaching so that they can guide others in achieving that vision.

The criteria for selection of mentors are important. There needs to be a well-defined selection process that adheres to the stated criteria so that teachers perceive that the process is fair and that it will result in the selection of highly qualified individuals. Most experts suggest that the criteria for selecting mentors be a part of the program design and aligned with the goals of the program. Mentors themselves need to understand the selection criteria and be clear about what it is they will be expected to do for and with the novice teacher or teachers assigned to them. Likewise, novice teachers need to understand what role the mentor will play and how the advice of the mentor will be made available to them.

Important mentor characteristics include the following:

- Approachability
- Integrity
- Ability to listen
- Sincerity
- Willingness to spend time
- Enthusiasm
- Teaching competence
- Trustworthiness
- Receptivity
- Willingness to work hard
- Positive outlook
- Confidence
- Commitment to the profession
- Openness
- Experience in teaching
- Tactfulness
- Cooperativeness
- Flexibility

DeBolt (1989)

The National Commission on Professional Development and Support of Novice Teachers suggests that the selection criteria be published so that everyone is clear about the mentor-selection process. This Commission also suggests that program sponsors agree on the length of experience that mentors should bring to the mentoring process. Mentors should be

- Committed to studying and developing their own practice.
- Able to model the standards-based teaching that the program is attempting to foster.
- Able to work with adults from diverse backgrounds.
- Sensitive to the viewpoints of others.
- Informed about mentor responsibilities and willing to make the necessary commitment to carry out these responsibilities, including a substantial time commitment.
- Committed to ethical practice.
- Committed to providing both professional and emotional support and challenge.
- Have completed the previously agreed-upon required number of years of teaching. (Odell & Huling, 2000, p. 20)

Exhibit 4.1 Selection Criteria for Support Providers

Selection criteria are consistent with the support provider's specified roles and responsibilities, including, but not limited to, the following:

(i) Knowledge of beginning teacher development;

(ii) Knowledge of the state-adopted academic content standards and performance levels for students, state-adopted curriculum frameworks, and the *California Standards for the Teaching Profession;*

(iii) Willingness to participate in professional training to acquire the knowledge and skills need to be an effective support provider;

(iv) Willingness to engage in formative assessment processes, including non-evaluative reflective conversations about formative assessment evidence with participating teachers;

(v) Willingness to share instructional ideas and materials with participating teachers;

(vi) Willingness to deepen understanding of cultural, ethnic, cognitive, linguistic, and gender diversity;

(vii) Effective interpersonal and communication skills;

(viii) Willingness to work with participating teachers;

(ix) Demonstrated commitment to personal professional growth and learning; and

(x) Willingness and ability to be an excellent role model.

Source: Excerpted from California Commission on Teacher Credentialing (2002). *Standards of Quality and Effectiveness for Professional Induction Programs.* Sacramento, CA: Author.

The selection criteria for mentors (support providers) in the *California Standards for Induction Programs* emphasize this role that mentors play and the knowledge, attitudes, and skills that they need in order to perform this important role. These guidelines link the criteria for selecting mentors to an understanding of not only the mentoring role, but of the vision for teaching and learning that has been adopted by California. Exhibit 4.1 outlines the criteria suggested in these standards.

Too often, mentors are chosen without enough care and attention to who is best fit for the role. They are assigned to the role for the sake of convenience or because it is their turn to be in the role. Or perhaps they take on the role simply for the extra stipend attached to it.

The selection process is not always carefully considered when a school or district has to match large numbers of beginning teachers with mentors. The primary concern in this case may simply be to find enough individuals who are willing to take on the role. Although willingness is an important criteria, merely being willing and available is not sufficient. One must possess the relevant skills or have the potential to learn those skills.

Experienced teachers who serve as mentors need to understand their roles and be prepared for their responsibilities. Most high-quality

Exhibit 4.2 Suggested Topics for the Professional Development of Mentors

- Observing and analyzing the practice of novices, with emphasis on profession standards-based teaching
- National and local reform initiatives to enhance teaching
- Collecting classroom data
- Communicating and resolving conflict
- Understanding novice development and the needs/concerns of novices
- Fostering productive conversations about teaching and learning
- Studying the mentor's own teaching and helping the novice learn from these processes
- Analyzing the learning of diverse students and helping the novices learn from these processes
- Mentoring strategies and practices to support and challenge novices to learn at their maximal level
- Analyzing school and district contexts and their influence on mentoring, teaching, and learning to teach
- Working with novices as adult learners
- Exploring ways to facilitate the novice's use of school, district, and community resources

Odell and Huling (2000, p. 20)

programs develop a training program for mentors. Exhibit 4.2 lists some suggested training topics.

In some ways, good mentoring is related to good teaching—teaching that enables students to take responsibility for their own learning. Mentors should learn to guide new teachers in identifying and solving their own problems and also guide them to reflective teaching practice. Some mentors want to intervene too quickly and solve the problem for the new teacher. Others avoid giving any suggestions for fear of sounding too critical. Mentors need to be coaches, guides, and facilitators. Mentors need to learn and practice the skills that are associated with effective mentoring (see Exhibit 4.3).

Mentors should understand that some new teachers are more receptive to help than others. Some new teachers struggle more than others. Their needs differ. Mentors need to learn to take cues from the new teacher and adapt their approach to meet the need the needs of the individual.

A primary goal of the mentor is to help new teachers become reflective about their own practice and to take responsibility for their own growth and learning. If the mentor is successful, the new teacher will gradually rely less on the mentor and will seek out new ideas and approaches on their own.

The mentor needs to learn to set boundaries and protect his or her own time. Because many mentors give out their home telephone numbers and e-mail addresses, they will find that questions from a particular needy teacher may intrude upon their own work and their own lives. Mentors need to speak up when this happens and be able to suggest alternative ways for the teacher to find the help the teacher needs.

Exhibit 4.3 Mentoring Skills

- Brokering relationships
- Building and maintaining relationships
- Coaching
- Communicating
- Encouraging
- Facilitating
- Goal Setting
- Guiding
- Managing conflict
- Problem solving
- Providing and receiving feedback
- Reflecting

Zachary (2000)

Many resources are available to help in the design of a training program for mentors and for mentors themselves to use to further their own development. Some suggested resources are listed at the end of this chapter.

MATCHING MENTORS TO NEW TEACHERS

It is important to consider the match of mentors and those new teachers they will be assisting. Compatibility of the mentor and new teachers is important to developing a good relationship.

Many new teachers prefer that their mentors work at the same grade level or in the same subject area so that they have a better understanding of the content of the curriculum that they will be teaching. However, mentors sometimes work successfully with teachers across disciplines and grade level. Proximity of work location can be helpful. A teacher who works next door rather than across town will probably be able to interact on a more regular basis with the new teacher. Age and gender sometimes play a factor in considering appropriate matches, but are probably less important considerations.

Most important is the "fit" between mentor and protégé. Daresh (2003) speaks of what makes for a good fit, suggesting that

> The ideal matching of mentors and protégés should always be based on an analysis of professional goals, interpersonal styles, and the learning needs of both parties. It is nearly impossible in the real world to engage in such perfect matching practices. Most mentoring relationships will likely be formed as marriages of convenience and not as the ideal naturally developing partnership that are so often presented in the literature. (p. 41)

It is helpful to gather some background information about the mentor and to make thoughtful matches. Information about teaching styles, personality characteristics, and preferences can be gathered from those who have knowledge of the individuals or through interviews or questionnaires.

TIME FOR NEW TEACHERS AND MENTORS TO WORK TOGETHER

Teachers and their mentors need time to work together. Some programs have the funding available to be able to release experienced teachers from the classroom to be full-time mentors to a number of beginning teachers. However, not all program have the resources to be able to do this. Mentoring programs all struggle with finding ways to make appropriate time available. Some approaches include

- Releasing teachers from classrooms for a portion of the day or week.
- Scheduling regular meeting times before or after the school day.
- Using staff development days for meetings.
- Meeting during lunch.
- Holding Saturday meetings.
- Scheduling common prep times for teachers and their mentors.
- Meeting during times that classes may be working with specialists.
- Hiring a roving substitute to cover classes when teachers are released.

Whatever arrangements are made, it is most important that regular meetings be scheduled and that teachers honor the established schedule. Many programs ask for documentation of these meetings to ensure that they do occur on a regular basis.

In addition to these meetings that allow for planning, discussion, and sharing of ideas, it is important that mentors have time to get into the new teacher's classroom to observe and give feedback to the new teacher. New teachers also find it helpful to observe their mentor or other experienced teachers. The mentor may want to take over the new teacher's class to demonstrate certain teaching strategies or may want to suggest that the new teacher visit another teacher's classroom.

These observations should be purposeful, and may be structured by some focusing questions so that the new teacher knows what observe. For example, the mentor may suggest such things as

"Watch to see how I handle transitions between lessons so that students remain attentive."

"Look for the different approaches I use to address this learning goal."

"Watch how Ms. Gonzales sets up her cooperative learning groups."

"See how Mr. Edwards modifies this lesson for his full inclusion student."

Teachers will benefit most from observations of others if they are looking for something specific. Focused observations give them that opportunity to first observe and then discuss what they have learned with their mentor (see Exhibit 4.4).

MENTOR COMPENSATION

In the most well-established, enduring programs, mentors are compensated for the work. They may be released from their own teaching duties on a full-time or part-time basis, or they receive a monetary stipend for their work performed in addition to their regular classroom duties. Some places that give a stipend to nationally board-certified teachers choose to use them in a mentoring role.

The amount of compensation ranges according to the funding level of the program. The payment should reflect the amount of time the mentor is expected to give to the role and the number of new teachers that teacher is assigned. Compensation needs to be at a level that is deemed significant so that mentor will take the responsibility seriously and make it a priority.

In addition to monetary compensation, mentors should receive recognition for their contributions to the profession. In some places, celebration dinners or ceremonies help to provide a way to publicly recognize the work that mentors perform.

MENTOR GROWTH AND DEVELOPMENT

Those who have studied the impacts of mentoring indicate that mentors often gain as much as the novice does from the relationship. In reflecting with new teachers, experienced teachers often are required to examine their own practice in a more thoughtful and critical way. They are called upon to explain what they do and why they do it in a certain way.

Mentors also indicate that the training they receive to serve in the role also increases their own understanding of practice. For many who have been teaching for a number of years the opportunity to learn about the latest educational ideas and practices is invigorating.

Mentors also learn from each other. The most effective programs offer opportunities for continued meetings and discussions among mentors. In those discussions, mentors share their successes and challenges and continue to focus on their own development.

Exhibit 4.4 Focused Observation Guide for New Teachers

What is to be observed:

_____ Teaching methods
_____ Classroom management strategies
_____ Student engagement and behaviors
_____ Role of teacher
_____ Lesson structure
_____ Teacher questioning strategies
_____ Allotment of time to instructional activities
_____ Teacher interaction with parent volunteers, paraprofessionals
_____ Grouping arrangements
_____ Other: _____

Date and time of observation:

Description of what was observed:

Reactions and comments:

Implications for practice:

Questions for further discussion with mentor:

Teachers who have been through a thoughtful program of induction have established habits of mind that lead them to continue to seek new and better ways of teaching. They want to continue to develop and hone their skills. They question what and how their students are learning. They continually examine their own practices. They begin to look for leadership roles in their professional lives.

Finally, those new teachers who are well mentored often become mentors themselves. The mentoring relationship has been modeled for them and they gradually gain the experience and skills to not only become expert in their own teaching, but able to help others experience that same success. They have become reflective about their own practice, and are now able to help others with that reflection.

A PLAN FOR THE MENTORING EXPERIENCE

Because mentoring is highly individualized, it is important to develop a plan for each teacher. In California, that plan is called the Individual Induction Plan (IIP). Others might refer to it as an action plan or by some other designation.

The plan is most useful if the new teacher, in careful consultations with the mentor, develops it. It includes professional growth goals and outlines specific strategies for achieving those goals. It offers a vehicle for documenting the teacher's progress in meeting those agreed upon goals. The teacher and the mentor will review the plan a on a regular basis and may be revise the goals or the plan as needed. Exhibit 4.5 presents an outline for the plan that is used in many of the induction programs in California. This plan builds on the California Standards for the Teaching Profession (CSTP) in defining goals for the new teacher. (These standards are discussed more fully in Chapter 6.)

INTENSITY OF MENTORING PRACTICES

Mentoring practices vary across and within programs. In some cases mentoring has a significant impact for the new teacher. In others, it is perfunctory and not as valuable.

Early research on the induction experience in California found that mentoring needed to be of a significant level of intensity in order to be effective in producing desirable changes in beginning teaching practice (California Commission on Teacher Credentialing & California Department of Education, 1992). Pilot projects were classified as low, medium, and high in mentoring intensity, depending on a number of criteria that have been discussed in this chapter and which are outlined in Exhibit 4.6.

Exhibit 4.5 Individual Induction Plan

(Review your IIP's and your progress toward your goals as you plan your next steps)

Teacher First Name: _____ Last Name: _____ District: _____

Support Provider First Name: _____ Last Name: _____ Date: _____

I. CSTP TEACHING STRENGTHS Based on evidence gathered in prior events, which elements of the CSTP describe my strengths as a teacher?	**2. CSTP TEACHING NEEDS** Which elements or CSTP standards will I focus on to improve my teaching?
3. GROWTH GOAL Considering the CSTP standard and elements I will focus on, my professional growth goal is . . .	**4. STUDENT OUTCOMES** Based on my CSTP growth goal, what changes could I see in my students?

5. IMPLEMENTATION PLAN
What will I do step by step to achieve my goal?

Start Date	Action	Evidence	Completed? Date	**6. RESOURCES THAT SUPPORT MY GOAL**

Individual Induction Plan

FORM DISTRIBUTION: WHITE – Project   YELLOW – Support Provider   PINK – Participating Teacher

CFASST 1.0

Page 1 of 1   Rev. 7/02

84

Exhibit 4.6 Intensity of Mentoring Support

Low-Intensity Mentoring	Medium-Intensity Mentoring	High-Intensity Mentoring
Selection criteria for mentors are not identified. Teachers volunteer to be mentors.	Mentors are selected by seniority, convenience, or by principal recommendation.	Mentors are selected by a committee according to well-defined, published criteria.
Experienced teacher has no special training in working with new teachers.	Mentor is given some training to work with new teacher (i.e., one day) and has had some prior experience in staff development.	Mentor completes extensive training in working with new teachers and continues to meet with other mentors throughout the year.
Mentor has no release time to work with new teachers.	Mentor has limited number of release days to work with each new teacher (e.g., one to five days per year).	Mentor is released full-time from own classroom to work with no more than fifteen new teachers, or mentor is released one half-day or full day to work with no more than four teachers.
Mentor is located at different school site than the new teacher.	Mentor works in the same school as the new teacher or in a school or nearby.	Mentor released part-time is located at same site as the new teacher and has taught in the same subject area or grade level as the new teacher.
Mentor teaches at different grade level or different subject areas than the new teacher.	The mentor meets with the new teacher at least once a week during lunch, after school, or during a free period.	The full-time release mentor is assigned teachers who are concentrated in a limited geographical area.
Mentor meets once a month or less with the new teacher.	Mentor has some knowledge of or experience with the curriculum being taught by the new teacher.	Mentor is compensated at a level that is considered fair a appropriate to the time commitment.
Mentor lets new teachers identify their own problems or issues for discussion.	Teachers agree on what constitutes good teaching practice.	A clearly articulated vision of teaching guides the mentoring process.
Concept of teaching is guided by individual beliefs, styles, and practices.	Mentor bases conversations with new teacher on observations of teaching or informal identification of needs and priorities.	Mentor conversations with the new teacher are based upon classroom observations and assessments of the new teacher's performance.
Little or no monetary compensation provided to the mentor.		

Although all induction programs in the pilot projects improved retention rates of new teachers, new teachers who experienced high-intensity mentoring made the most dramatic gains in teaching performance. They were most likely to exhibit teaching performance that is typically associated with higher levels of student achievement, For example, they used a wider variety and greater complexity of teaching strategies, were more focused on individualizing instruction, and exhibited more ability to use strategies appropriate to diverse student populations. In other words, they moved along the continuum of teacher development faster than those who did not experience this degree and level of support.

High-intensity mentoring certainly is the most desirable if we wish to reach the established goals for the induction programs. It is also the most costly in terms of resources. However, induction programs that make this commitment to high intensity mentoring find that is a cost-effective approach because the time and resources spent to retain and develop the skills of a fully prepared teacher more than offset the costs of hiring and retraining new teachers (California Commission on Teacher Credentialing et al., 1992).

MENTORING CHALLENGES

Not every mentoring relationship is successful. There are some challenges to developing and maintaining good mentoring relationships. Some of these challenges are described below.

Identifying sufficient numbers of appropriate mentors. Even after the criteria are defined, it may be difficult to identify enough appropriate experienced teachers who are willing to serve as mentors. Increasingly, experienced teachers are reluctant to be away from the own classrooms to work with novices. Those who are identified as possible mentors may not be located at the same school sites as new teachers. In these cases, it is often difficult for teachers to get together on a regular basis or to observe one another teach.

> None of the mentors have a P.E. background, so it doesn't exactly work for me. It was 10 weeks before he even introduced himself to me. Then all he ever did was ask, "So how is it going?" I get more help from the other P.E. teachers. We work as a team.
>
> Second-year teacher

Matching mentors to new teachers. Most programs attempt to match mentors with new teachers who are teaching at the same grade level or in the same content area. Some believe that it is desirable to find a mentor at the same school site as the new teacher, so the novice has regular contact with the mentor. However, these matches are not always possible to make. Sometimes there is a personality conflict between mentor and new teacher; or perhaps they subscribe to very different teaching styles and approaches. When there is a conflict or problem with the relationship, a change in assignments may be warranted.

> My mentor was not too helpful with my biggest problem—classroom management. She just said, "You are going to develop your own style."
>
> First-year teacher

Time constraints. The intensity of the mentoring program makes a difference in how effective it will be. However, it is often difficult to find enough time in the workday to allow mentors and their new teachers to plan, observe in each other's classrooms, and to have the kind of in-depth conversations that make for rich mentoring. Programs that are funded at a sufficient level can provide for release time or pay teachers for their work outside of the regular workday.

Even those who have sufficient resources to provide for release time often find that experienced teachers hesitate to be away from their own classrooms on a regular basis. They are concerned about the learning of their own students. Administrators and parents also express concerns about pulling the excellent teacher out of the classroom too often. There may even be a shortage of qualified substitute teachers to fill in when the classroom teacher is away.

Despite these obstacles, there are many benefits to be gained from making time in the day for intensive mentoring. All participants need to make mentoring a priority in already very busy schedules.

MENTORING THE UNDERPREPARED TEACHER

Too often, mentors fail to distinguish between teachers who have been fully prepared and those who are still in the midst of their preparation programs. Special attention needs to be given to mentoring of the under-prepared or alternate-route teacher.

Mentoring should begin with an assessment of what the new teacher already knows, understands, and is able to do. Even fully prepared teachers will bring different ideas and practices to their first teaching assignment. When alternate-route teachers first enter classrooms, they often lack very basic knowledge about how to manage classrooms, how students learn, and what needs to be taught.

When teachers enter classrooms without the benefit of a preparation program, many school districts will provide some training in what is often called "survival pedagogy." A typical range of topics covered in this introduction are outlined in the one-week training program that is offered to beginning teachers in the Los Angeles Unified School District who are entering the profession in a alternate-route program. The program provides some very basic training as well as an introduction to the district (see Exhibit 4.7).

Exhibit 4.7 Teacher Training Academy Certification Curriculum

---

For: General Education Teachers, Special Education Teachers, and Substitute Teachers

Module One: What do you know about how children learn?
  Creating a classroom community
  Knowledge traditions in education
  Collaboration
  Introduction to Los Angeles Unified School District
  Schools of all children
  California standards for the teaching profession
  Stages in the learning-to-teach continuum
  Teacher certification unit
  Learning theories
  District demographics
  Diverse learners
  Least-restrictive environment
  Individualized Education Plan (I.E.P.)
  Diversity: How diverse am I?
  Introduction of the participant portfolio

Module Two: What should children know and be able to do?
  Reflective journals
  Types of journals
  Classroom discipline
  Creating a classroom community
  Content standards for California public schools
  Assessment
  Writing a rubric
  Assessing student writing
  Student Success Team/Language Appraisal Team
  Preparation for classroom observation
  Cambourne's Conditions of Learning

Module Three: How do I instruct all students?
  Debrief of school visitations
  Demonstration lesson
  Differentiation in the classroom
  Categories of students

Lesson planning for diverse learners
Eligibility categories for students with special needs
Los Angeles Unified School District services
Culturally responsive teaching
Academic English Mastery Program (AEMP)

Module Four: What will a typical day/week look like?
Learning styles
Multiple intelligences and learning styles
Bloom's taxonomy
Teaching language arts
Elements of reading
Understanding reading instruction
Important reading skills
The writing process
District reading program
English Language Development Instruction (ELD)
Teaching Math
Teaching Social Studies
Teaching Science
Teaching Physical Education
Teaching Visual and Performing Arts
Special Education break-out session

Module Five: What else do I need to know about teaching in the LAUSD?
Nine Principles of Learning
Special education issues
Los Angeles Unified School District policies
School forms
Family involvement
Long-range planning
Substitute teacher plans
Phases of the first-year teacher

Source: Teacher Training Academy Certification Curriculum for General Education Teachers, Special Education Teachers, and Substitute Teachers. Publication 633, Los Angeles Unified School District, Revised July 2002. Human Resources/Alternative Certification Unit.

Alternate-route teachers find this introduction to be quite useful in helping them begin their work (Bartell, 2004). However, this is, indeed, only "survival-level" information and there is still much to be learned. Much of what is presented in these early sessions will be developed and expanded upon later in the alternate-route teachers' formal programs of study and further induction and support experiences.

It is quite appropriate that such mentoring is focused on the survival level. Alternate-route teachers will need additional help and mentoring with these basic skills as they begin their work. Their mentors need to anticipate and understand these survival-level needs.

Most alternate-route teachers continue to take courses in the evening, on weekends, or over the summer. Coursework, while often useful, is sometimes perceived as too theoretical to meet the beginning teacher's immediate survival needs. If a mentor is aware of what the new teacher is studying, the mentor may be able to help the new teacher interpret and apply that learning to the classroom. The mentor can also provide invaluable assistance in helping the new teacher become more knowledgeable credential program requirements. Although the alternate-route teacher probably has been advised about these requirements, the credential requirements are often quite complex and confusing. Advising of the alternate route teacher is not always as thorough and well informed as it is for those who take the more traditional path.

While traditional route students focus first on their preparation and then on putting that preparation to into practice, the alternate route teacher must focus on both simultaneously. The challenges of learning to teach while actually teaching can be overwhelming. Mentors working with alternate route teachers need to recognize what is most needed and focus first on those needs.

Taking courses concurrently with beginning a teaching career adds to the stress of beginning teaching. Survival needs mare magnified for the teacher who enters the profession in this manner. Mentors can help new teachers unburden and cope with that stress by being a listener, a guide, and a friend. They can also encourage by helping show the way to more accomplished teaching.

IMPLICATIONS FOR PRACTICE

The main points of this chapter and their implications for practice can be summarized as follows:

1. Mentors can play a key role in the induction program.

2. Mentoring is professional practice that occurs in the context of teaching whenever an experienced teacher supports, challenges, and guides novice teachers in their teaching practice.

3. Mentoring is most effective when it is guided by a vision of excellent teaching and is focused on helping to improve instructional practice.

4. Mentors should be carefully selected according to established criteria.

5. Careful attention should be given to matching mentors and new teachers so that they are compatible.

6. Time needs to be set aside for mentors and new teachers to work together on a regular basis. There should also be an opportunity for mentors and new teachers to observe one another as they teach.

7. Observations should be structured or focused so that they are most beneficial.

8. Mentors should be compensated appropriately for their time and recognized for their contributions. It often causes experienced teachers to become more reflective about their own work.

9. A written plan for each individual new teacher's growth and development can help to guide the induction experience.

10. High intensity mentoring is most likely to achieve the desired results.

11. Challenges to mentoring in some contexts include
    - Insufficient numbers high-quality mentors.
    - Poor matching strategies.
    - Time constraints.
    - Insufficient resources.

12. Special attention needs to be given to mentoring the alternate-route teacher who is most likely to struggle with a number of survival-level issues.

FOR FURTHER READING

Daresh, J. D. (2003). *Teachers mentoring teachers: A practical approach to helping new and experienced staff.* Thousand Oaks, CA: Corwin.
This book gives practical advice about planning and implementing a mentor program. The author indicates that mentors can be used for veteran and new teachers alike, and suggests ideas for both cases. Guidelines are suggested for developing benchmarks for measuring progress of the mentoring plan.

Graham, P., Hudson-Ross, S., Adkins, D., McWhorter, P., & Stewart, J. M. (Eds.). (1999). *Teacher/mentor: A dialogue for collaborative learning.* New York: Teachers College Press.
This book is the collaborative effort of a group of teacher educators, middle and high school teachers, and preservice teacher candidates. They work and write together as they engage in collaborative inquiry. The book focuses on mentor teacher–teacher candidate relationships, teacher research; teacher challenges; and building an educational collaborative community. All are teachers of language arts/English.

Jonson, K. F. (2002). *Being an effective mentor: How to help beginning teachers succeed.* Thousand Oaks, CA: Corwin.
This is a useful guide to help mentor teachers develop effecting mentoring strategies, including how to provide direct assistance, demonstration teaching, observation and feedback, informal contact, and role modeling. It also includes a monthly listing of activities designed to promote interaction between the mentor and protégés that correspond to activities and events occurring during the typical school year.

Odell, S. J., & Huling, L. (Eds.). (2000). *Quality mentoring for novice teachers.* Indianapolis, IN: Kappa Delta Pi.
The National Commission on Professional Development and Support of Novice Teachers, a group of experts convened by the Association of Teacher Educators in collaboration with Kappa Delta Pi produced this mentoring framework to guide, assess, and develop effective mentoring programs. It identifies ways in which quality mentoring can enhance school cultures in which standards-based teaching is the focus. The Mentoring Framework is illustrated with vignettes that serve as rich examples of the mentoring process.

Portner, H. (2002). *Mentoring new teachers.* Thousand Oaks, CA: Corwin.
Portner shows teacher mentors how to (a) relate to their protégés in ways that establish good working rapport; (b) assess how the mentoring is progressing and make necessary adjustments; (c) coach protégés to help them continually improve their performance; and (d) guide protégés from dependence on their mentors to self-reliance as effective teachers. The book includes specific activities and exercises to teach mentors behaviors that elicit trust, help them become more effective at the mentoring process, and methods for boosting protégés' day-to-day effectiveness in the classroom.

Rowley, J. R., & Hart, P. M. (1999). *High-performance mentoring kit: A multimedia program for training mentor teachers.* Thousand Oaks, CA: Corwin.
This is a complete training package for preparing veteran teachers to be effective mentors. It includes a facilitator's guide with detailed descriptions of twenty-five individual workshop modules, including training objectives, materials needed, and recommended instructional strategies. It also includes videotapes, a CD-ROM with PowerPoint slides, and a participant notebook. Facilitators will be able to help participants to
- Reflect on the mentoring process.
- Explore problems and concerns of the beginning teacher.
- Adapt their mentoring practices to the developmental needs of their mentees.
- Deliver quality interpersonal support.

Rudney, G. L., & Guillaume, A. M. (2003). *Maximum mentoring: An action guide for teacher trainers and cooperating teachers.* Thousand Oaks, CA: Corwin Press.
This book provides support to those who serve as mentors of preservice or beginning teachers. Offering step-by-step guidance to mentoring, this book includes many practical suggestions about how to help teachers explore and reflect on their own practice. It includes coverage of rules, roles, relationships, responsibilities, and procedures used in mentoring.

Zachary, L. J. (2000). *The mentor's guide: Facilitating effective learning relationships.* San Francisco: Jossey-Bass.
This book approaches mentoring from the perspective of adult learning. The book includes stories, tips, strategies, and tools for the mentor. It covers the full range of the mentoring process: assessing readiness; establishing a relationship; setting appropriate goals; monitoring progress; avoiding pitfalls; and bringing the relationship to a natural conclusions.

5

Urban Schools and Induction

Induction programs hold special promise for urban schools where teacher turnover is high and student achievement is in need of improvement. While the features of effective induction programs are common across all settings, the program elements need to be adjusted to meet the particular needs of the urban context. Induction in the urban context needs to be a part of broader reform efforts. This chapter discusses the particular challenges of induction in urban settings and offers suggestions about how to deal with those challenges.

INDUCTION AND THE URBAN SETTING

Doolittle, Herlihy, and Snipes (2002) remind us that school reform efforts are fundamentally about improving urban public schools. They make a compelling case for this attention:

> The 100 largest school districts, most located in urban areas, serve 23 percent of the nation's children. The nation cannot afford to ignore these communities, for urban schools enroll a large share of America's children. While there are 16,850 public school districts in the United States, one hundred of those districts serve approximately 23 percent of the nation's students. These districts, many of

which are located in urban areas, also serve 40 percent of the country's minority students and 30 percent of the economically disadvantaged students. (p. 1)

The numbers, as well as the enormous learning needs of our urban students, demand that we prepare, nurture, and develop teachers who are able to provide a high-quality educational experience to all learners. Yet, there are some challenges to educators who are serious about improving the educational experience in urban settings. Urban schools are often characterized by the following historical and contextual factors that tend to thwart reform efforts (Doolittle et al., 2002; Cibulka, Reed, & Wong, 1992):

- Unsatisfactory academic achievement
- Political conflict
- Inexperienced teaching staff
- Turnover of administrators
- Low expectations and lack of demanding curriculum
- Lack of instructional coherence
- High student mobility
- Poor facilities in unsafe neighborhoods
- Racial, ethnic, and cultural mismatch of teachers and students

Urban induction programs face all of the same contextual challenges that plague other reform efforts. However, the induction movement holds special promise for urban schools where the need to attract and retain well-qualified teachers is essential to school improvement efforts. The contextual challenges are discussed in the following sections with special emphasis on what these challenges mean for induction in the urban setting.

UNSATISFACTORY ACADEMIC ACHIEVEMENT

Student standards and expectations have established high expectations for achievement. However, by almost any measure, student achievement in our central cities has for too long lagged behind that of the nation. This disparity especially impacts poor and minority students who are noticeably behind white and more affluent students.

New teachers enter urban schools with high hopes of making a difference for their students. However, beginning teachers often lack the ability to diagnose or remediate learning problems and deal with students who need special assistance just to catch up. Curriculum materials are usually focused on typical grade-level expectations and it takes a skilled teacher to adjust or modify curriculum to fully engage students in learning at their level of understanding.

This is coupled with the need to serve the increasing number of English-language learners who are concentrated in our urban schools.

New teachers are often unskilled in making adaptations to the needs of students who come from many cultures and language backgrounds.

Beginning teachers in urban settings need a special focus on student achievement to help close the gaps in students learning. They need help in matching learning experiences to the needs and abilities of their students and need support and encouragement in their efforts. They need models and the mentorship of experienced teachers who hold high expectations for their students and are able to help their students achieve those expectations. They need site administrators who hold high expectations for the teaching staff and for the students at their schools. They need the support of dedicated, committed educators who not only believe that all students can learn, but work to ensure that learning does occur.

POLITICAL CONFLICT

The politics of educational decision making in large, urban settings can be discouraging and frustrating to new and experienced teachers alike. Political conflict arises over matters of curriculum, budgeting, facility planning, salaries, taxes, public relations, student assignment, desegregation plans, and almost any other important issue related to schooling. Cities are especially hard hit in times of declining resources and dwindling tax bases, and are increasingly impacted by the flight of the more affluent to the suburbs.

The politics of large city schools often result in shifting priorities and commitments among competing interests. Mayors of the larger cities are playing an increasing role in school governance, further politicizing the schools. School boards often represent a collection of special interests, rather than a unified vision of what is best for schools.

Reform efforts, including the implementation of induction programs, are highly dependent on leadership support and sustained commitment. Turnover in leadership often means a change in focus and reform initiatives. Induction programs, unless built into the structure of the district, are likely to get lost among many competing priorities and agendas.

Teacher induction programs need to be free of political conflict and competing agendas. All interests will be well served by a strong program that transcends local politics and is focused on a sustained effort to introduce teachers to the responsibilities and rewards of teaching in urban schools.

INEXPERIENCED TEACHING STAFF

Teacher turnover is higher in urban schools than in any other setting. Urban schools have more difficulty attracting and retaining certified teachers that have completed a state-approved preparation program and demonstrated their knowledge and the ability to teach. When there is a shortage of well-qualified teachers, credentialed and experienced teachers choose to teach in what they consider more desirable locations. Urban schools are more likely to hire persons who have little or no formal preparation but strong desire and potential then to encourage enrollment in an alternative preparation program.

Last-minute hiring is a characteristic of the large bureaucracies in urban settings. Teachers are often assigned to classrooms shortly before they begin teaching. There is little time for them to prepare for their specific assignment or for a decent orientation to the procedures and practices of the school and the district.

Teachers in urban schools are more likely than those in other areas to be underprepared for beginning their careers; they often begin to teach before they earn a credential. Teachers who lack the appropriate credentials are not the preferred choice of those responsible for hiring new teachers; they are most often hired out of necessity.

These underprepared teachers are generally more tentative about their commitments and are more likely than fully qualified candidates to leave the profession. However, even certified teachers are more likely to leave urban schools if other opportunities are presented to them. Because urban schools have enormous staffing needs, the high turnover rate among teachers in these settings can have particularly devastating effects when trying to build a strong, committed cadre of educators to serve students.

In many urban schools, up to a third of the teaching staff are beginning teachers in their first three years of teaching. Among these beginners, few will be fully prepared academically. The demands for support and mentoring are much greater than they would be in a comparable suburban school that has only a few new, fully qualified teachers to support. It is difficult to find the needed numbers of highly qualified mentors in urban settings who are willing, capable, and available to offer the intensive mentoring described in Chapter 4 of this book.

Urban schools need to be committed to recruiting, hiring, and then retaining the educators who are likely to be successful in urban settings. Induction programs designed to improve teacher retention will help to address the teacher turnover rate, foster improved retention, and offer opportunities for more experienced teachers to play a leadership role as mentors.

TURNOVER OF ADMINISTRATORS

Just as the turnover of teachers in urban schools is higher than in non-urban schools, there is also a higher turnover among administrators, both at the district office level and at the site level. Turnover is highest at the top level. The Council of Great City Schools reports that the average tenure of the superintendent in big-city schools is 2.75 years.

With leadership change comes a change in curriculum and program focus. It is difficult to sustain any long-term focus or direction without continuity of leadership. The current superintendent's reform efforts replace those of his predecessor on a regular basis.

There is generally a shortage of individuals in the pipeline who want to assume site-level leadership. The shortage of well-qualified school administrators is most acute in urban settings. As was indicated in Chapter 3, strong administrative leadership and support is essential to support and sustain high-quality induction programs.

Induction programs need to enlist administrative support to promote continuity in program delivery and to make induction a priority. A strong induction program that becomes a part of the culture can transcend the turnover in leadership if it becomes integral to the way new teachers are brought into the system. Induction should be a natural next step after the teacher is hired.

LOW EXPECTATIONS AND LACK OF DEMANDING CURRICULUM

Teachers become frustrated and discouraged when the academic expectations seem way beyond the capabilities of their students. Too often they lower their own expectations for their students in the belief that they are matching the ability level of the students. They offer a less-demanding curriculum than is presented elsewhere.

New teachers need to be encouraged to hold high expectations for their students and to provide a rigorous, challenging curriculum. They need to truly believe that their students are capable if presented challenges in appropriate ways. They also need to be surrounded by colleagues who are highly motivated and committed to the students they serve. They need to be supported by mentors and by administrators who will help them understand how to best reach and teach their students.

Rather than make excuses for low performance, teachers need to be encouraged to focus on the goals outlined in the curriculum standards and translate those standards into appropriate instructional strategies and practices.

Let me tell you, these new teachers struggle with real, live students with more than their share of problems every day. They want to know how to get students to turn in homework. They want to know what to do with students are in seventh grade but read at a second-grade level. They could care less about Vygotsky.

Principal

LACK OF INSTRUCTIONAL COHERENCE

Teachers in urban settings have become inundated with reform efforts. Just as they master one curricular innovation, it is discarded in favor of another. It is hard to sustain commitment to such reforms if teachers know they are likely be asked to implement yet another approach or strategy.

Instructional improvement efforts need long-term, sustained commitment if they are to have any lasting effect and impact on learning. Teachers need to see that commitment so that they are encouraged in their own efforts to implement the plan. Many educators have become jaded by so many false starts and shifting priorities.

Induction programs need to incorporate and support the local reform agenda, but only if it is a long-term reform. Induction programs themselves need to have that same long-term commitment if they are to be successful. They need to be a part of a cohesive, integrated, long-term instructional improvement effort.

New teachers need to see models of good teaching that achieve desired results. Induction programs that are successful will identify and attempt to replicate best practices, those that are found to be successful in the urban setting.

HIGH STUDENT MOBILITY

Urban settings are often characterized by patterns of high student mobility. Students relocate and lose continuity in their own learning. Beginning teachers need to know how to address this mobility and how to help students integrate into their new settings. They need to help students feel welcome and adjust to their new classroom environment.

High rates of student mobility call for the ability of teachers to quickly diagnose the needs of students and to provide opportunities to fill the gaps that may result from a changed learning situation. Induction programs can help new teachers understand the social, psychological, and educational needs of students who are highly mobile and may lack strong family and community support.

POOR FACILITIES AND
UNSAFE NEIGHBORHOODS

Urban schools are more likely to be in disrepair and be situated in blighted neighborhoods. It is hard to convey enthusiasm in an environment that seems to convey the opposite. Teachers become disillusioned and discouraged by the conditions under which they work. They are often not comfortable living or spending time in the community. Urban teachers often have concerns about their own safety and the safety of their students.

Urban schools often have inadequate instructional resources to support learning. Teachers and their students do not have adequate numbers of textbooks, library materials, and teaching materials that are often available elsewhere. The technology gap has widened the disparity in resources between the rich and poor schools. Students in urban areas lack the computers in the schools and in their homes that their suburban counterparts have come to expect to have as a basic learning tools.

Our urban schools need to address the issue of workplace conditions in order to attract and retain a high-quality teaching force. They need to look for the support to provide appropriate learning resources. They need to ensure the safety of students and the teachers who work there.

Other schools I have visited seem to have more materials—more books and lots of computers.

First-year teacher

TEACHER-STUDENT MISMATCH

Another factor that impacts induction practices in urban settings is the mismatch of race, language, and cultures among teachers and their students. White, middle-class individuals continue to dominate the teaching profession. Students in urban settings are predominately poor and are children of color. This makes it particularly challenging for teachers to identify with their students, relate to their parents, and to understand their experiences and lives. It is difficult for students to identify with their teachers or the learning experiences that are presented to them by teachers who do not appear to be like them or to understand them.

Urban schools are populated with large numbers of English-language learners who are likely to be working below grade level. While English-language learners are found in nonurban settings as well, the numbers and diversity of language backgrounds in the urban setting are likely to be much greater. Even well-prepared teachers are not always ready to deal with the learning needs of students who have difficulty with learning in a language that is not spoken in their homes.

All teachers need to be prepared to work with the students they will encounter. While this diversity faces most teachers in the United States today, the greatest range of diversities and the largest mismatch between the culture of the teacher and the cultures of students is found in urban schools. This should be a key focus of the teacher induction program.

> The teacher turnover rate in urban schools is much higher than suburban schools. . . . The result is that urban schools, especially those in the inner cities, are often staffed largely by newly hired or uncertified teachers. These teachers, who were trained to teach students from middle-class families and who often come from middle-class families themselves, now find themselves engulfed by minority students, immigrants, and other students from low-income families—students whose values and experiences are quite different from their own.
>
> Crosby (1999, p. 302)

THE CASE FOR TEACHING IN URBAN SETTINGS

Despite these challenges, many new teachers do choose begin their careers in an urban setting. One study (Bartell, 2004) indicated that teachers choose to work in these settings for the following reasons:

- They are from the community and want to "give back"
- They want to make a contribution to the betterment of society
- They live in the community and it is convenient to work at a school nearby
- They are attracted to the alternate-route program that allows them to enter teaching without a full credential

For the most part, urban teachers are idealistic and want to make a difference in the lives of children. These teachers need support so that they will remain and so that they and their students will be successful.

> I graduated from this school. I want to "give back" to my community.
>
> Second-year teacher

Recruitment, retention, and induction efforts need to be thought of as connected. Urban schools should build upon the motivations and commitments that drew the beginning teacher into an urban setting in the first place.

Those who already live or have lived in the community or have attended a university in the area are a strong pool of potential recruits. Those who have studied alternate-route teachers also indicate that familiarity and comfort with the urban setting is a strong predictor for future success in that setting (Haberman, 1996). Strong recruitment programs that match these individuals with preferred locations will allow them to work near home and they are more likely to be motivated to remain.

Alternate-route teachers are often attracted to urban settings because of the ease of entry and the ability to earn a living teaching while learning to teach. This route into teaching is especially attractive to those who may be strong candidates but lack the resources to take time off and go back to school full-time.

Those individuals with altruistic motives need to be encouraged and supported in their commitments to "make a difference." Their mentor might continue to help them focus on what they are doing that has positive result. Barriers to their efforts should be removed. These teachers need colleagues who share their perspectives and a school culture that supports their efforts.

Alternate-route teachers who come for the opportunity to learn while working as a teacher need to have a good experience so that they decide to remain even after they finish their program of studies. Their induction program should help them see their work as more than temporary, but as an opportunity to make a long-term commitment.

Teachers often come to urban schools because they have deep commitments to perform a service to society and make a difference in the lives of the students they teach. These teachers need to be supported in their efforts to do so. They need to feel a sense of professional efficacy and a satisfaction with their work. They need feedback from others that indicates that they are, indeed, making a difference. They need to experience success.

While the urban setting has its special challenges, there are some who seek an urban setting because of the diversity and opportunity it offers. Ingersoll (2001) points out that that urban schools offer more diversity, flexibility, academic freedom, and career options for teachers. He reminds us that "simply by virtue of their size, large schools and large school systems may also offer more job and mobility opportunities for teachers either within the school or within the district" (p. 527). Urban environments can offer an exciting, dynamic and diverse living environment, rich with cultural and entertainment advantages. This appeals to many who can be enticed to come and may offer incentives to remain.

Urban districts need to intentionally accentuate the advantages and positive aspects of working in an urban environment. At the same time, district planners need to recognize and deal with the barriers to good teaching and learning that were highlighted at the beginning of this chapter. Teachers who see the rich opportunities and experience success may be encouraged to remain and make a long-term contribution. Those who are supported in their intentions to live out their commitments are more likely to make a lasting contribution to their students, their schools, and their communities.

INDUCTION IN THE URBAN SETTING

Most urban districts recognize the need for the type of induction program described in this book. Fideler and Haselkorn (1999) report that 81% of the nation's largest school districts have felt the need to initiate induction programs of some type. In their study of induction practices in urban schools nationwide, the following were identified as barriers to inductee success:

- Inadequate classroom management skills
- Disruptive students, discipline problems
- Difficulty organizing time and work schedule
- Inadequate instructional skills
- Unfamiliarity with the curriculum
- Isolation in the classroom
- Insufficient preparation for dealing with cultural diversity
- Difficult setting/low-performance school

While these sound like the same needs of new teachers in other settings, the challenges of the urban setting accentuate and magnify the needs. Induction programs can personalize the support and mentoring that new teachers receive in the vast, impersonal bureaucracies that often characterize urban schools. They can provide support and encouragement in situations where teachers are most likely to become discouraged. They can help teachers learn more about their students' cultures and their learning needs. They can help teachers develop the skills and expertise to be effective teachers in the context of their urban settings.

Induction programs for urban schools will be most successful if they include all of the induction components discussed in Chapter 3. However, these features need to be tailored to the context of the urban setting.

These components of effective induction programs across all settings are reviewed in the first column of Exhibit 5.1. Because these elements become more complex in urban settings, the exhibit also outlines, in the second column, the implementation issues for urban schools.

Implementation challenges are related to the challenges of the character of urban education discussed earlier. The sheer numbers of new teachers that need induction services in urban schools make the task appear to be quite daunting. The turnover of administrators in urban schools also contributes to a lack of continuity in leadership and support for induction. New teachers enter teaching at many points on the continuum of preparation, from having no formal coursework to being a fully prepared teacher. There are many competing professional development and reform efforts underway in most urban schools, which compete for the time and energy of teachers and teacher leaders. Teacher mentors or leaders often have many other responsibilities in addition to their classroom duties and mentoring. Administrators are reluctant to release the best teachers from classroom duties to help other teachers when the needs of students are so great. The large, impersonal nature of urban schools makes collegial work more of a challenge.

Many urban districts are finding ways to overcome these challenges to establish and support strong induction programs for their new teachers, with very positive results. Programs in Cincinnati, Rochester, Albuquerque,

Exhibit 5.1 Considerations for Implementation of Induction Programs in Urban Settings

Program Features	Considerations for Urban Schools
Purpose and goals	Purposes aligned with special needs of local urban schools to attract and retain teachers. Goals aligned with goals for students.
Intended outcomes	Outcomes specified in terms of district goals and learner outcomes.
Leadership and administration	Leadership crucial to support and maintain in large urban district with many competing interests and programs.
Collaboration	Large urban districts will require strong collaborative efforts among many groups and organizations and regular communication among providers of services to new teachers.
Support of site administrators	Large urban districts also have more administrator turnover. New school leaders need to be informed and prepared for their roles to ensure program continuity.
Linkages with university preparation	Partner with all local universities to ensure they are preparing teachers for understanding and working in urban schools.
New teacher assignment	Teachers will need to understand and be ready to work successfully in the urban context. Training should focus on successful strategies in urban settings.
Context	It is difficult to find release time for new and experienced teachers because of the lack of qualified substitutes. Careful scheduling may be required.
Mentoring	Many well-prepared mentors will be needed to serve the large numbers of new teachers beginning their work in urban settings. Mentors should be models of effective urban practices.
Provision of scheduled, structured time	Release time for follow up by mentors may present special challenges. On-site mentors facilitate more frequent contact and better conversations among teachers.
Professional development	Teachers in urban settings enter at various stages in their training. Professional development needs may be greater and fall within a wider range of readiness to teach.
Individual follow-up	Follow-up activities should be geared to the needs of teachers and the students in their own particular setting.
Feedback to beginning teachers	Time for reflective discussion needs to be built into the schedule and feedback should be geared to specifics of successful practices in urban settings.
Evaluation	Evaluation should be focused on the goals established for the urban setting.

Jefferson County, Los Angeles, San Diego, Minneapolis, Norfolk, Clark County, and Chicago were profiled by Fideler and Haselkorn (1999). These researchers who found that the districts they visited all featured "orientation, training, and support for new teachers, but these components differ widely with respect to frequency and duration of contact, reach (i.e., percentage of eligible inductees served), and delivery method.

These are not the only urban districts giving attention to the induction years. Many others, especially when induction is a statewide endeavor, have developed or are developing induction programs and trying to find the resources to keep them running, even during a time of budget reductions. They are doing this because they know that the quality of the teacher workforce will make the biggest difference in the educational programs in urban schools.

We have much to learn about induction in urban settings from those who are making strong efforts to give vital attention to the support of their new teachers and from the efforts to evaluate those programs. The most successful efforts have been those that have been sustained and supported over time and have been attuned to the needs of their particular new teachers.

TEACHERS FOR DIVERSE URBAN SCHOOLS

Diversity in the student population is not confined to urban settings. Most university preparation programs now include some preparation to work with diverse populations of learners. However, most urban principals and those responsible for who hiring new teachers indicate that such preparation is often insufficient for teachers who have had little or no experience in an living or working in urban environments.

Racial, ethnic, cultural, and socioeconomic diversity are primary characteristics of most urban environments. With a more diverse population comes a wider variety and diversity of learning needs. Teachers need to understand and appreciate their own students' culture, their perspectives, and their experiences. They need to see diversity as a strength that offers richness to our schools and to our society. They need to learn how to address the ever-widening and expanding needs of the children they serve. They need to believe that all students are truly capable of learning at a high level, and that it is up to educators to find ways to ensure that students have equal access to educational opportunities.

> I've found classes valuable that deal with cultural diversity and theories of language acquisition. Those are pretty big for me because I really like thinking about theory and then applying that to my experience in my school.
>
> Third-year teacher

Those who work in and study urban schools indicate that successful urban teachers possess special characteristics. Zeichner (1993) identified the following as characteristic of an effective urban teacher: high expectations for students, a strong self-identity, use of a variety of teaching methods, an understanding of the community, and an advocate for justice. Learning to teach and reach all children in our multicultural society is an ongoing process that needs attention at each phase of the teacher's development.

The dispositions of teachers toward their students heavily influence their instructional practices. Stoddard's research (1993) found that "teachers who feel different from their students and who negatively evaluate that difference are unlikely to develop or use culturally sensitive curriculum and instructional practices" (p. 47). These teachers make little attempt to adapt their curriculum to the needs of diverse learners or to offer learning experiences that challenge them in significant ways. They simply do not believe students are capable. On the other hand, Stoddard indicates that "teachers who feel comfortable in urban multicultural environments appear to be much more supportive and sensitive to the needs of inner-city students" (p. 47). These teachers give their students assignments that require and stimulate higher-order thinking, believing that they are can achieve if they are challenged and supported in their learning.

> The needs of these students are really different than the mainstream. What they get at the school is it. Their parents are supportive, but a lot of them don't have the ability to help in reading and writing. They are English-language learners and a lot of the students are coming into an English-only class for the first time. . . . And then you have the disadvantages that come along with poverty. Kids may live in a one-bedroom house with ten other people. They don't have a quiet place to read. They don't have the parents that may support their learning.
>
> Second-year teacher
> (Achinstein & Barrett, 2003, p. 12)

The expectations that teachers have for their students makes a vast difference in the kinds of tasks and the level of challenge presented to them. Adapting instruction to the needs of diverse learners too often results in providing a less-challenging, less-engaging curriculum. Students will not learn to deliberate, to think critically, or to become analytic if they are not given opportunities to learn in this way.

Effective teachers in the urban schools are those who seek to challenge and engage their students and believe that their students can succeed. They understand the barriers to learning, and seek to remove them or to lessen their impact. They know what teaching methods work and don't work with their students. They understand their own students and are able to connect learning with their students' lives and experiences. They adjust curriculum to meet needs without "watering down" what they offer. They find the way to motivate and to help students to engage and to learn.

To be effective, teachers need to connect learning to the lives and experience of students. In a diverse, urban setting, this means that the curriculum is culturally responsive to the students and that it includes

- Materials and resources that reflect students' cultural values, history, and beliefs derived from students' interests and curiosities.
- Classroom experiences designed to encourage a connection between students' lives and the principles they study.
- Reading resources that match students' developmental levels— particularly the needs of second-language learners.
- Tools to help students assert and accentuate their present and future powers, capabilities, attitudes, and experiences.
- Teacher behaviors that demonstrate respect and understanding for students' cultural and ethnic backgrounds and socioeconomic conditions.
- Teacher recognition and support for differentiated learning.
- Selection of curricular materials that encourage the development of thinking processes, particularly research skills, analytical thinking, and problem solving. (Brown, 2002, p. 113)

TOWARD CULTURAL PROFICIENCY

Many advocate that we prepare and nurture teachers so that they become culturally competent, to help them understand and appreciate cultural differences. Lindsey, Nuri Robins, and Terrell (2003) argue that mere competence is no longer enough; instead, the more proactive "cultural proficiency" is needed. By "cultural proficiency" they mean that educators need to respond to diversity with more than mere tolerance or acceptance; they need to see the differences and respond in a positive and affirming way. This means "esteeming culture, knowing how to learn about individual and organizational culture, and interacting effectively in a variety of cultural environments" (p. 6). This work is guided by five key principles that describe culturally proficient behavior:

- Assessing culture
- Valuing diversity
- Managing the dynamics of difference
- Adapting to diversity
- Institutionalizing cultural knowledge

For the teacher, the principles of cultural proficiency are lived out in the classroom as indicated in Exhibit 5.2.

Exhibit 5.2 The Culturally Proficient Teacher

Assess culture	Assess own culture and its effect on students Assess the culture of classroom Support students in discovering their own cultural identities
Value diversity	Teach all subjects form a culturally inclusive perspective Insist on classroom language and behaviors that value differences
Manage the dynamics of difference	Use conflict as object lessons Teach students a variety of ways to resolve conflict
Adapt to diversity	Learn own instructional and interpersonal styles Develop processes to enhance them sop that they meet the needs of all students Help students to understand why things are done in a particular way
Institutionalize cultural knowledge	Teach students appropriate language for asking questions about other people's cultures and telling other people about theirs

Source: Lindsey, Nuri Robins, & Terrell (2003), p. 119.

Cultural proficiency is a goal for all who are going to work in contemporary schools, but has particular relevance for those who work in urban settings. Too often, teachers take a deficit approach to educating those who are not like them. The goal is to make them fit into the mainstream rather than to teach and learn with them about who they are their place in the world. Cultural proficiency is reflected in the way each person who has a place in the school community—administrators, students, teachers, staff, and parents—is treated with dignity and respect. In a culturally proficient organization, the culture of the organization promotes inclusiveness and institutionalizes processes for learning about differences and for responding appropriately to differences. Rather than lamenting, "Why can't *they* be like *us?*," administrators, teachers, staff, parents, students, and the community welcome and create opportunities to better understand who they are as individuals, while learning how to interact positively with people who differ from themselves.

Cultural proficiency is a goal for individual teachers, as well as for the entire school organization that nurtures and supports their development and their work. If teachers are inducted into a particular organizational context, that context ought to encourage cultural proficiency.

MENTORS FOR URBAN SCHOOLS

Chapter 4 discussed the role that mentoring plays in teacher retention and in the development of teaching skills, abilities, and perspectives.

Mentoring the urban teacher calls for experienced teachers who not only are successful themselves in the urban context, but are able to help the newcomer understand, grow, and thrive in this context.

Urban mentors need to be guides to reflective practice in the urban context. Although mentors in urban schools may need to possess some of the same characteristics and qualifications as mentors elsewhere, they may also need to have a special set of qualities for effective mentoring in their particular setting.

Haberman (1994) believes that teachers grow professionally in urban schools by being associated with "star" teachers. He indicates that these stars are often a product of the urban schools themselves, and characterizes these teacher-leaders as those who can do "gentle teaching in a violent society" (p. 3).

> An urban pedagogy must be built on the strengths of the city, the hope and promise of kids and families, on the capacities of city teachers. We must create an enjoyable teaching experience and a classroom life that teachers want to be a part of. . . . Urban classrooms must be places where teachers can pursue their ideas, explore their interests, follow their passions—and be engaged with students in living lives of purpose.
>
> Ayers and Ford (1996, p. 214)

Guyton and Hidalgo (1995) suggest the role of mentor in an urban environment is a unique one, and that the mentor should be a change agent, an efficacious teacher, a collaborator, have a clear sense of self, be a pedagogue with diverse cultural perspectives, and have strong interpersonal skills. Careful selection and training of mentors is essential so that new teachers are presented models of good teaching in the urban context.

Developing, Nurturing, and Supporting the Mentors

The challenge in urban schools that are heavily populated with many newcomers is to find a cadre of seasoned professionals. As was discussed in Chapter 4, mentors themselves need to be carefully selected, prepared for their roles, and nurtured and supported themselves. This is especially important in the urban setting.

Mentoring itself may be more challenging in the typically large and often impersonal environment of urban schools where the environment itself is not often nurturing or supportive. Induction programs need to select carefully for potential for mentoring and then develop mentoring skills in those potential "stars."

Teachers who show potential for leadership are often tapped to become mentors. A mentor-development program can be established to help these individuals gain the necessary and vital skills associated with strong and effective mentoring.

As noted earlier, bringing mentors together on a regular basis to discuss their mentoring work has great value. Teachers who are professionals seek like-minded colleagues to stimulate and enrich their own thinking. Mentors in urban schools can learn from each other and support one another in their efforts. They need this colleagueship in their own schools and with successful mentors in other schools and their professional organizations and activities.

Mentoring for the urban mentors pays off in the long run. Mentors learn from each other, are encouraged by the experiences of one another, and form their own communities of practice. They learn to examine their own teaching practices and mentoring practices with others in a reflective way. Because they are in a leadership role, they can often play a key role in not only helping the new teacher succeed and remain in that setting, but also in helping to change the culture of the school.

Being an urban mentor may, in fact, be the professional challenge that a more experienced urban teacher seeks. Urban mentors are teacher-leaders that ought to be valued, rewarded, and recognized for their work.

MERGED PREPARATION AND INDUCTION

Another challenge for induction in urban schools is the large number of teachers who are inducted before they have completed their initial preparation to teach. Teachers entering the profession through alternate routes are most commonly found in the largest numbers in urban settings.

Because the concept of induction for teachers was formulated and developed primarily for teachers who were already academically prepared, the alternative-route teacher has not often been considered in the design of induction activities. Sometimes they are not even included in the induction program, or are formally inducted after they complete their initial credential requirements, which could be quite a few years. Chapter 2 alluded to the problems of neglecting to plan appropriately for the alternate route teacher.

A recent external evaluation of the Beginning Teacher Support and Assessment Program in California indicated that

> BTSA officials have tried to keep the focus of their program on new fully credentialed teachers. This approach is understandable, given the original design of the program. However, the unintended consequence of this policy is that the new teachers who need the most support—underprepared teachers—receive the least support. . . . Failure to address the induction needs of a growing majoring of new teachers in California is not a realistic option for the long-term health of the BTSA program. (Tushnet, Briggs, Elliot, Esch, Haviland, Humphrey, et al., 2002, p. 146)

This same study found that the induction activities were being undermined in districts with large numbers of new, underprepared teachers and that the program itself was "largely irrelevant" to these alternate route teachers.

Alternate-route teachers, particularly interns who are involved in a formal program of study, taking one or two classes while they teach, seem ill-suited for both the content of the induction program that builds prior knowledge and makes more demands on their already scarce time. They find additional observations, meetings, workshops, and other activities to be overwhelming rather than supportive. They are often getting too many directions from too many different people.

When a new teacher participates in a preparation program and an induction program simultaneously, it is important to stage the learning experience carefully so it can be of most benefit to the new teachers. Mentoring and professional development needs to be offered in a timely way and should be integrated with the course learning whenever possible to provide a consistent and coherent program of support and development for the teacher.

Induction plans, just as teaching plans, need to accommodate learners at all levels. The solution proposed is to develop a "merged model" of preparation and induction that is staged appropriately to the teachers' needs and level of development. This takes careful planning and communication between the organizations and individuals providing both preparation and induction services. The program is individualized, through carefully induction planning, to the stage and level of development of the teachers. Teachers should not be overwhelmed with "help" that is inappropriately staged or is more intrusive than helpful.

I had four observers in my classroom just in the last two weeks. My intern supervisor was here. My mentor came to see my first period class because I am having some management problems with that one. The team from "Learning Walk" came. My assistant principal came to evaluate me. You (the researcher) are the fifth. It's a little too much help!

Second-year teacher

The various providers of training (usually the district and the university) need to work together to better plan and deliver this merged program. If district planners are aware of the university's requirements, they can even use the mentoring to help their teachers understand and meet those requirements. Lesson plans and assignments developed for courses can be implemented in the classroom under the tutelage of the mentor, forming the basis of reflective conversations between novice and mentor.

University programs can do a better job of offering and tailoring programs to the needs and schedules of teachers, offering what they need when it will do the most good, and using the teacher's own classroom as a laboratory for that teacher's learning.

Alternative-route programs will remain a viable option for many teachers and will probably continue to grow as the need for staffing continues. These alternatives predominate in many urban settings, but are being used quite extensively in other settings as well. It is important to make these options strong and to ensure that teachers meet all the same standards that are met by those in more traditional programs.

> You know I was complaining about the philosophy of learning class, but it kind of makes teaching seem like a real profession. It forces you to think about all the different theories. So I really appreciated that one after I took it. It was tough to get through—a lecture from 7–10; I was tired. But, I learned a lot and really appreciated it after it was over.
>
> Third-year teacher

A merged program of preparation and induction need not shortchange either the preparation or induction experience. In fact, the learning that is a part of preparation can have immediate follow-up with application to the teacher's classroom setting under the guide of the mentor.

Alternate-route teachers, like their more traditionally prepared colleagues, should learn to be reflective in their work. It is important that alternate-route teachers be well supported in their preparation/induction years so that they, too, will become successful teachers over time. When induction programs are individualized to meet the needs of the new teacher, the alternate-route teacher's needs will be met.

IMPLICATIONS FOR PRACTICE

The main points of this chapter and their implications for practice can be summarized as follows:

1. Challenges to school reform that make good induction programs more challenging in the urban setting, include
   - Unsatisfactory academic achievement.
   - Political conflict.
   - Inexperienced teaching staff.
   - Turnover of administrators.
   - Low expectations and lack of demanding curriculum.

- Lack of instructional coherence.
- High student mobility.
- Poor facilities in unsafe neighborhoods.
- Racial, ethnic, and cultural mismatch of teachers and students.

2. Recruitment, retention, and induction efforts need to be thought of as connected. Urban induction programs should build upon the motivations and commitments that drew the beginning teacher into an urban setting in the first place.

3. Induction programs in urban settings particularly need to help teachers overcome
   - Inadequate classroom management skills.
   - Disruptive students and discipline problems.
   - Difficulty organizing time and work schedule.
   - Inadequate instructional skills.
   - Unfamiliarity with the curriculum.
   - Isolation in the classroom.
   - Insufficient preparation for dealing with cultural diversity.
   - Difficult setting/low-performance school.

4. Features of successful induction programs in general apply to induction programs in urban settings. However, special consideration needs to be given to how to successfully implement those features in the urban context.

5. Successful induction practices in urban schools ought to be examined and shared with others.

6. Racial, ethnic, cultural, and socioeconomic diversity are primary characteristics of most urban environments. Teachers need to be prepared and mentored to work effectively with diverse populations, whether in urban or nonurban schools.

7. Effective teachers in the urban schools are those who are culturally proficient, who seek to challenge and engage their students, and who believe that their students can succeed.

8. Careful selection of mentors is essential so that new teachers are presented models of good teaching in the urban context.

9. Urban mentors learn from each other, are encouraged by the experiences of one another, and form their own communities of practice.

10. A "merged model" of preparation and induction should be developed for alternate-route teachers, who are most often found in urban schools.

FOR FURTHER READING

Ayers, W., & Ford, P. (Eds.). (1996). *City kids: City teachers.* New York: New Press.
This is a collected work of essays and memoirs that speak to the teacher's urgent mission to engage the urban learner. In this book, students and teachers share their problems, their prospects, and their plans. It begins with the voices of students. It contains a section of thoughtful commentary on some of the critical issues facing teachers: language, race, class, culture, violence, and poverty. It concludes with the voices of teachers and their accounts of classroom life.

Brown, D. F. (2002). *Becoming a successful urban teacher.* Portsmouth, NH: Heinemann.
An experienced urban educator shares his own practical advice and the stories of thirteen experienced teachers about how to establish a comfortable learning environment for urban students. Special attention is given to describing specific tactics for
- Assisting students who are reading below grade level.
- Addressing differences in ability.
- Fitting in with veteran faculty.
- Satisfying local administrators.
- Handling the pressure of standards.

Cattani, D. H. (2002). *A classroom of her own: How new teachers develop instructional, professional, and cultural competence.* Thousand Oaks: Corwin.
Close to 80% of all new teachers are young, white, and female. When these teachers are assigned to urban settings, they face challenges of working with many at-risk students and are vulnerable to challenges based on age, power, experience, authority, race, class, and gender. The book follows their on-the-job struggles and achievements as they develop confidence and competence in instructional, professional, and cultural realms.

Fideler, E. F., & Haselkorn D. (1999). *Learning the ropes: Urban teacher induction programs and practice in the United States.* Belmont, MA: Recruiting New Teachers.
This is a report of a national study conducted by Recruiting New Teachers, Inc. It includes a discussion of induction's recent history followed by a report of the findings of a survey of 118 respondents in 35 states. Respondents were asked about the features and characteristics of their urban induction programs. Ten urban district programs are profiled in in-depth case studies.

Knapp, M. S., & Shields, P. M. (Eds.). (1991). *Better schooling for the children of poverty: Alternatives to conventional wisdom.* Berkeley, CA: McCutchan.
This book presents and synthesizes current research-based thinking about effect academic instruction in elementary schools that serve high proportions of students from impoverished backgrounds. It focuses not on "remediation" but on more appropriate forms of instructional practices. The book contains chapters by leading scholars in the field.

Shulman, J. H., & Mesa-Bains, A. (Eds.). (1993). *Diversity in the classroom: A casebook for teachers and teacher educators.* San Francisco: WestEd.
This casebook includes thirteen compelling first-person accounts of inner-city teaching dilemmas, focusing on the teacher–student relationship in multilingual, multicultural, and multiethnic classrooms. The narratives provide stimulation for group discussion by both teachers and professional developers.

6

Standards-Based Teaching and Reflective Practice

Induction programs that seek to move teachers beyond the survival stage engage teachers in a critical look at their own practice and the learning of their students. Standards for teachers and students help to define a vision to guide teacher reflection in the induction program. This vision encourages reflective practice among teachers. This chapter focuses on the concept of standards-based, reflective practice and its contributions to development of teaching in the early years and beyond.

INDUCTION FOCUS

Early induction programs focused mainly on providing support for new teachers so that they would not become discouraged and would remain in the classroom. These programs addressed the procedural, managerial, and psychological needs that were outlined in Chapter 1 (see Exhibit 1.1). Although it is essential that these needs be addressed, it is shortsighted to limit the scope of the induction program to these basic survival needs.

While teacher retention is still a goal of most programs, many realize that those initial goals were too modest. The potential to shape emerging practice cannot be ignored. As Feiman-Nemser (2003) states, "When we meet their learning needs, new teachers can reach their full potential—not only by staying in the profession but also by improving learning for all students" (p. 29).

Today the most thoughtful induction programs give attention to the procedural, managerial, and psychological needs of teachers, and also focus on their instructional, professional, cultural, and political needs as outlined in Exhibit 1.1. This expanded focus on the range and depth of what it means to be a teacher is more likely to help that teacher move beyond survival toward highly successful practice and expertise.

The most effective induction programs help new teachers understand and support the learning and success of all of their students. In such programs, teachers develop a sense of professionalism and a view of the larger context for learning in these initial years. They come to understand their students—what they know and do not know and how they learn. They begin to understand the larger cultural and political context in which they work, and the impacts those contexts have on student learning. The guidance they receive is based on a vision of excellence that helps teachers critically reflect on their own work, their practice, and the progress of their students.

This kind of teaching develops over time and must be considered in the everyday life of the classroom context. It cannot be reduced to simple formulas or strategies, but is highly dependent on the actions of teachers and teacher interactions with students. It demands that teachers be guided by a rich and complex vision of teaching and that they become reflective about their practice. This is a view that that recognizes the teacher as a successful professional.

THE CONCEPT OF REFLECTIVE PRACTICE

The term *reflective practice* has been so overused that it has almost become a cliché. Preservice and practicing teachers alike seem to be faced with many exhortations to reflect on their work. As one preservice teacher indicated, "I've been doing so much reflecting, I feel like a walking mirror" (Treiman, Mahler, & Bartell, 2000).

The reflection in a mirror presents an image of one's self that may be examined and scrutinized. To be reflective about what one is doing is to give that act some thoughtful consideration rather than to perform it in a routine and unexamined way. One dictionary definition of reflective is "characterized by deep, careful thought."

> I think too that one thing that really helped me was that my support provider, she would never give it to me, the information. She would make me think.
>
> First-year teacher
> (Storms & Lee, p. 2001, p. 33)

Teaching that is reflective is done in a deliberative, thoughtful manner that is hardly routine or formulaic. Reflective teachers make conscious choices and are able to articulate why they make those choices. They examine and scrutinize their own practice. They analysis of the students' work and their progress and adapt their instructional approach based on that analysis.

Because we know that teachers make about 200 decisions every school day (Clark & Peterson, 1986), it is hard to imagine a teacher who does not engage in some form of reflection as the teacher goes about her work. In fact, some would maintain, "there is no such thing as an unreflective teacher" (Zeichner, 1996).

Others think that teacher reflection ought to be made more explicit and intentional. The roots of this reflective approach to teaching can be found in the work of Dewey. In his book, *How We Think: A Restatement of the Relation of Reflective Thinking to the Educative Process*, Dewey indicated that reflective thinking is important because it "converts action that is merely appetitive, blind, and impulsive into intelligent action (1933, p. 17). If teachers are going to get their students to think in a critical, reflective way, they must model reflective practice themselves.

Our more contemporary vision of reflective practice is grounded in the work of Schön (1983), who introduced the educational community to a compelling vision of reflective practice that involved a critical process of refining one's artistry or craft in a specific discipline. He maintains that reflective teaching is, in part, largely intuitive and characterized by "reflection in action." By this he means that reflection often occurs quickly and in response to the immediacy of the situation. Schön argues that professional education ought to be centered on enlarging the practitioner's ability for informed problem solving throughout the professional's career.

> Every day I go home and reflect and say, "OK, what could I have done better?" It's not that you're going to think, "Oh, I'm going to do an inquiry now," but it's constantly reflecting (on) what I can do to get that kid engaged, because today he wasn't or she wasn't. . . . You don't have to think about it because it just happens.
>
> First-year teacher
> (McCormick, 2001, p. 66)

Schön (1987) uses the term *"professional artistry* to refer to the kinds of competence practitioners sometimes display in unique, uncertain, and conflicted situations of practice" (p. 22). He indicates that professionals need to learn more than the relevant facts, rules, and procedures associated with their chosen profession. The reflective practitioner develops the "forms of inquiry by which competent practitioners reason their way, in problematic instances, to clear connections between general knowledge and particular cases" (p. 39).

Schön's work and the work of others who wrote about the importance of teacher reflection prompted more attention to how teachers think about and enact teaching practice. It called into question the idea that teachers are mere "technocrats" and unthinking conformists who implement "teacher-proof" curriculum in standardized fashion. This growing body of work on teacher reflection has supported the belief that teaching is truly a profession and that teachers are decision makers and problem solvers who work in an extremely complex environment. Consider the following perspectives:

> The reflective teacher is one who is able to analyze their own practice and the context in which it occurs; the reflective teacher is able to stand back from their own teaching, evaluate their situation, and take responsibility for their own future action. (Calderhead, 1992, p. 141)

> Reflective teaching is teaching with careful thought and judgment. (Valli, 1997, p. 68)

> Reflection on teaching, on the effectiveness of both materials and teaching methods, shows promise in improving instruction. Examining what we do and how students respond seems critical to growth. (Fisher, Fox, & Paille, 1996, p. 417)

> Reflective time, whether alone or with a trusted coach or colleague, affords teachers an opportunity to analyze their work. By reflecting on their teaching, teachers can evaluate their impact on students, their priorities, their professional effectiveness, or their approaches to problems encountered with students. (Kent, 1993, p. 83)

> Reflection is an essential step in the lifelong process of learning from our personal and professional experiences. . . . Reflection is particularly valued in the context of a professional life, because of its potential to change learning while we are in the midst of professional practice. (Watson & Wilcox, 2000, p. 57)

STANDARDS FOR A PROFESSION

Reflection on practice will be most productive if it is guided by a rich conception of what that practice is about. Many think that teaching will become a more highly regarded profession if there are rigorous standards to guide the practice of that profession (National Commission on Teaching and America's Future, 1996). If we are to hold teachers to high expectations, we need to have an agreed-upon set of statements that describe what teachers ought to know and be able to do.

> I like the idea of the standards for teachers. It makes teaching seem like more of a profession.
>
> Second-year teacher

Over the past two decades, a number of groups at the state and national levels have worked to define what those standards ought to be. Such standards have been developed to give a focus to teacher preparation, induction, and continued professional development.

Many educators are increasingly nervous about this standards movement and view standards as an attempt by regulatory bodies to overprescribe the content, direction, and focus of teacher education and development programs. We are, indeed, in the middle of a standards movement that seems to compel uniformity and that narrows rather than broadens our sights. Despite the efforts of local, state, and national authorities to engage a large number of professional educators in the development, articulation, modification, and validation of those standards and expectations for teacher development, this movement often feels like a "top-down" rather than a "bottom-up" activity.

To standardize is to systematize or to make uniform. Standards may, in some forms, be narrow and prescriptive, aimed toward the lowest common denominator rather than reaching for the highest potential of teaching expertise. Educational systems that foster such prescriptive systems of accountability are what Elmore (1983) calls "compliance effecting" rather than "capacity enhancing."

Standards that seek merely to compel compliance are narrow, regulatory, and often highly specific. Such standards are quite specific not only in regard to intent, but in regard to how that intent should be realized. Narrow, compliance-oriented standards fail to recognize the complexity and the many dimensions of teaching expertise. Compliance-oriented standards are designed to ensure a minimum level of competence rather than to point to a vision of expertness that provides a goal for life-long learning.

But standards need not be so narrowly defined. Standards can be designed to empower and facilitate the building of capacity in teachers and their mentors to discover together the best way to meet the expectations for performance. Capacity-enhancing standards for teachers represent what we know from research and best practice. They define in broad terms what teachers should know and be able to do as they think critically about their practice.

Educators can play a significant role in designing and then interpreting standards in their own settings. These sorts of standards can build and enhance the capacity of teachers as they test them out, refine, extend, and give meaning to them in the context of practice. Capacity-enhancing standards invite and challenge teachers and teacher educators to engage in deliberative, reflective conversation about the best ways to meet the standards in their own particular settings with their own students. Such standards are designed to encourage teachers to aim for an expert level of performance, but recognize that there are many steps along the way and perhaps different paths to attainment.

Darling-Hammond (1997) writes about "creating standards without standardization," indicating that "standards ought to embody a general aim and vision for changes that must still be worked through in more specific terms in the schools. This working through process is educative in itself as it stimulates inquiry into practice" (p. 232).

STANDARDS-BASED INDUCTION

Standards-based induction practices are relatively new. Initial induction programs in the 1980s were focused primarily on providing support and encouragement to teachers, with no clear direction about the focus of that support or the content of the mentoring and professional development offered. Discussions about practice among new teachers and their support providers were highly idiosyncratic and grounded in individual beliefs about what constituted good practice. We had no common set of standards or expectations by which to measure teacher performance.

> The biggest challenge for me would probably be knowing what's the most important to teach of all of the standards and what to spend more time on and the best ways to teach it so it makes sense to eighth graders.
>
> First-year teacher

Today's educators begin their teaching in an accountability-driven environment that compels a focus on what teachers can do to increase student learning. Standards for students have made more explicit the outcomes for which teachers will be held accountable. It was a logical next step to assume that standards for students would be accompanied by standards for teachers. Darling-Hammond (1997) makes the point that standards for students and standards for educators are linked. She argues that

When students are expected to achieve higher standards, it stands to reason that educators must meet higher standards as well. They must know how to enable students to master challenging content and how to address the special needs of different learners. Therefore high and rigorous standards are a cornerstone of an accountability system that focuses on student learning. (pp. 245–246).

Professional standards need to become the basis for planning induction programs. Standards give teachers and their mentors the common language to discuss, guide, develop, reflect on and assess their practice.

> The CSTP [California Standards for the Teaching Profession] helps me have those good conversations with teachers about what they are doing in the classroom and where they need help. I meet with new teachers and their mentors each month. The standards remind us what is important and keep us all on track.
>
> Assistant principal

There are excellent model standards for beginning teaching at all levels—local, state, and national. Two such efforts to specify empowering, capacity-enhancing standards that seek to capture the complexities of teaching are described here. One was a national effort and the other was a state effort. Both are used or adapted for use in many teacher-preparation and induction programs.

NATIONAL STANDARDS
FOR BEGINNING TEACHERS

In 1987, the Interstate New Teacher Assessment and Support Consortium (INTASC) was established to enhance collaboration among states interested in rethinking teacher assessment for initial licensing as well as for preparation induction into the professional. Under the sponsorship of the Council of Chief State School Officers, a national task force worked to develop standards that would embody the kinds of knowledge, skills, and dispositions that teachers need to practice responsibly. Over a period of eighteen months, representatives from seventeen states met on a regular basis to draft, refine, and pilot test in their own states the standards that were intended to serve as model standards for states to adopt, adapt, or guide the development of standards in their own states. State representatives pilot tested these standards extensively among teachers in their own states.

The INTASC Standards (outlined in Exhibit 6.1) are grounded in a common core of teacher knowledge that outlines "foundations of practice

Exhibit 6.1 The INTASC Principles

Principle #1: The teacher understands the central concepts, tools of inquiry, and structures of the discipline(s) he or she teaches and can create learning experiences that make these aspects of subject matter meaningful for students.

Principle #2: The teacher understands how children learn and develop, and can provide learning opportunities that support their intellectual, social and personal development.

Principle #3: The teacher understands how students differ in their approaches to learning and creates instructional opportunities that are adapted to diverse learners.

Principle #4: The teacher understands and uses a variety of instructional strategies to encourage students' development of critical thinking, problem solving, and performance skills.

Principle #5: The teacher uses an understanding of individual and group motivation and behavior to create a learning environment that encourages positive social interaction, active engagement in learning, and self-motivation.

Principle #6: The teacher uses knowledge of effective verbal, nonverbal, and media communication techniques to foster active inquiry, collaboration, and supportive interaction in the classroom.

Principle #7: The teacher plans instruction based upon knowledge of subject matter, students, the community, and curriculum goals.

Principle #8: The teacher understands and uses formal and informal assessment strategies to evaluate and ensure the continuous intellectual, social and physical development of the learner.

Principle #9: The teacher is a reflective practitioner who continually evaluates the effects of his/her choices and actions on others (students, parents, and other professionals in the learning community) and who actively seeks out opportunities to grow professionally.

Principle #10: The teacher fosters relationships with school colleagues, parents, and agencies in the larger community to support students' learning and well being.

Source: INTASC (1992).

that cut across specialty areas—the knowledge of student learning and development, curriculum, and teaching, contexts and purposes which create a set of professional understanding, abilities, and commitments that all teachers share" (INTASC, 1992, p. 2).

The INTASC Task Force recognized that teachers' assumptions, beliefs, and commitments are reflected in how they conduct themselves in the classroom and how they relate to their students. The INTASC standards describe not only knowledge that the teacher possesses, but also the performances that can be demonstrated and assessed, and dispositions or statements about teacher beliefs.

By 1997, at least twenty-four states adopted or adapted a form of these standards for their own use (Darling-Hammond, 2001). These states are using the INTASC standards to guide teacher development in the early years in both preparation and induction programs.

A fuller elaboration of the ten principles of the INTASC standards can be found online at www.ccsso.org. These standards are shaping preservice and induction programs nationwide. They can be useful to induction planners who currently have no standards guiding their programs or as a supplement to existing standards.

STATE STANDARDS: CALIFORNIA

While many states have adopted or adapted the INTASC Standards, other states have developed their own standards to guide teacher development in their preparation and induction programs. One state that began working on standards about the same time that INTASC was formed is California.

In 1988, California initiated the California New Teacher Project (CNTP), a pilot study of alternative methods of supporting and assessing teachers who were new to the classroom. The CNTP funded pilot projects, funded through competitive grant awards, to test alternative models for supporting and assisting the professional development of first-year and second-year teachers, and assessing their competence and performance in the classroom. From 1988 to 1992, thirty-seven local and regional pilot projects explored alternative, innovative ways of supporting and assessing more than 3,000 first- and second-year teachers. Over the entire 4 years, more than 3,000 beginning teachers and more than 1,500 experienced teachers participated in the CNTP. The pilot projects were the subject of a large-scale, multiyear external research and evaluation effort that formed the basis a statewide system of induction, or the Beginning Teacher Support and Assessment Program (BTSA).

Expansion of programs continued around the principles that had been established in the pilot studies. Although it was always the intent that the program would be offered to all beginning teachers, it would be 2003 before the state would require that all teachers participate in a planned induction program of support and assessment as a part of earning their professional-level credential.

One recommendation of the early induction studies in California was that a well-defined set of teaching expectations, or standards, should be developed to guide both the support and assessment components of future induction programs. As the BTSA program began its expansion to include more new-teacher participants throughout the state, a task force was formed to begin work on those standards. The work was pilot tested and validated in the gradually expanding BTSA program, and the adopted version had the input of thousands of educators throughout the state. The resulting standards, the *California Standards for the Teaching Profession* (CSTP) were adopted by all relevant policy-making bodies—the California Commission on Teacher Credentialing (CCTC), the California Board of Education, and the Superintendent of Public Instruction. (California Commission on Teacher Credentialing & California Department of Education, 1997).

While initially intended as a guide to induction programs, the California Standards have been embraced and used by a wide range of educators in the state. Many universities began to use them to shape the initial preparation program. Districts have used them to guide their redesign of teacher evaluation systems and their Peer Assistance and Review (PAR) programs for experienced educators.

Educators in California accept the CSTP as a definition of accomplished teaching. The standards present a framework for professional development in preservice, induction and beyond. They point to a vision of successful, expert teaching to which all teachers can aspire.

Exhibit 6.2 outlines the California Standards. The full set of standards, with reflective questions, can be found on-line at: http:ctc.ca.gov.

STANDARDS-BASED PRACTICE

Standards provide a common set of expectations and a common language for talking about excellence in teaching. They provide an impetus toward reflective practice and a basis for reflection. The INTASC Standards and the CSTP are examples of standards for teacher performance that encourage deep, thoughtful reflection about the work of teaching. Many states have developed their own standards that are similar to these two examples. Likewise, many professional organizations have considered and adopted standards to guide teaching practice.

Both the INTASC and the CSTP standards were an attempt to develop powerful, rich standards that would be standards that avoided standardizing in too narrow a sense. Developers of these standards recognize that individuals will interpret and shape the standards in the context of their own practice.

The INTASC Standards, the CSTP, and others like them were developed to give this rich, in-depth focus to the induction period for new teachers. Teaching standards have changed the way we think about working with new teachers who are on the path to becoming experts.

Exhibit 6.2 The California Standards for the Teaching Profession

STANDARD FOR ENGAGING AND SUPPORTING ALL STUDENTS IN LEARNING	STANDARD FOR PLANNING INSTRUCTION AND DESIGNING LEARNING EXPERIENCES FOR ALL STUDENTS
Teachers build on students' prior knowledge, life experience, and interests to achieve learning goals for all students. Teachers use a variety of instructional strategies and resources that respond to students' diverse needs. Teachers facilitate challenging learning experiences for all students in environments that promote autonomy, interaction, and choice. Teachers actively engage all students in problem solving and critical thinking within and across subject matter areas. Concepts and skills are taught in ways that encourage students to apply them in real-life contexts that make subject matter meaningful. Teachers assist all students to become self-directed learners who are able to demonstrate, articulate, and evaluate what they learn.	Teachers plan instruction that draws on and values students' backgrounds, prior knowledge, and interests. Teachers establish challenging learning goals for all students based on student experience, language, development, and home and school expectations. Teachers sequence curriculum and design long-term and short-range plans that incorporate subject-matter knowledge, reflect grade-level curriculum expectations, and include a repertoire of instructional strategies. Teachers use instructional activities that promote learning goals and connect with student experiences and interests. Teachers modify and adjust instructional plans according to student engagement and achievement.
STANDARD FOR CREATING AND MAINTAINING EFFECTIVE ENVIRONMENTS FOR STUDENT LEARNING	STANDARD FOR ASSESSING STUDENT LEARNING
Teachers create physical environments that engage all students in purposeful learning activities and encourage constructive interactions among students. Teachers maintain safe learning environments in which all students are treated fairly and respectfully as they assume responsibility for themselves and one another. Teachers encourage all students to participate in making decisions and in working independently and collaboratively. Expectations for student behavior are established early, clearly understood, and consistently maintained. Teachers make effective use of instructional time as they implement class procedures and routines.	Teachers establish and clearly communicate learning goals for all students. Teachers collect information about student performance from a variety of sources. Teachers involve all students in assessing their own learning. Teachers use information from a variety of ongoing assessments to plan and adjust learning opportunities that promote academic achievement and personal growth for all students. Teachers exchange information about student learning with students, families, and support personnel in ways that improve understanding and encourage further academic progress.

(Continued)

Exhibit 6.2 (Continued)

STANDARD FOR UNDERSTANDING AND ORGANIZING SUBJECT MATTER FOR STUDENT LEARNING	STANDARD FOR DEVELOPING AS A PROFESSIONAL EDUCATOR
Teachers exhibit strong working knowledge of subject matter and student development. Teachers organize curriculum to facilitate students' understanding of the central themes, concepts, and skills in the subject area. Teachers interrelate ideas and information within and across curricular areas to extend students' understanding. Teachers use their knowledge of student development, subject matter, instructional resources, and teaching strategies to make subject matter accessible to all students.	Teachers reflect on their teaching practice and actively engage in planning their professional development. Teachers establish professional learning goals, pursue opportunities to develop professional knowledge and skill, and participate in the extended professional community. Teachers learn about and work with local communities to improve their professional practice. Teachers communicate effectively with families and involve them in student learning and the school community. Teachers contribute to school activities, promote school goals, and improve professional practice by working collegially with all school staff. Teachers balance professional responsibilities and maintain motivation and commitment to all students.

Source: California Commission on Teacher Credentialing (CCTC) & California Department of Education (CDE). (1997). *California standards for the teaching profession*. Sacramento, CA: Author.http://www.ctc.ca.gov

These are not merely survival-level standards, but standards to guide and shape professional development and practice for a career of teaching.

Such standards set high expectations for teachers. However, teachers need to consider teaching standards as a companion to other standards and expectations for which they and their students will be held accountable. The teaching standards specify what teachers need to know and be able to do to enhance student learning for their particular students.

STUDENT STANDARDS

That schools are increasingly accountable for results has increased the pressure on new teachers along with everyone else. There is no "grace period" for new teachers that will allow for poor results while the teacher gains confidence and acquires skills. This makes the induction years more important than ever.

It is difficult to talk about standards for teachers without thinking about the learning standards for students. In the final analysis, teachers will be held accountable for student learning and for helping their students meet the standards that have been established for student learning in their states and in their schools.

> The principal here is awesome. She keeps us focused on the California Standards and emphasizes the use of rubrics in evaluating student work.
>
> Second-year teacher

Standards for students have developed rapidly as the pressure mounts to demonstrate measurable results in schools. Many educators have felt uncomfortable with the development of student standards, thinking they were narrowing the curriculum or, in some cases, trivializing the learning that needs to take place. However, policy makers and the public continue to demand that schools be held accountable for meeting those standards. Consequently, we need to help teachers understand, interpret, implement, and measure progress toward attaining the standards that have been established for their students.

A strong induction program will include an emphasis on standards and expectations for students. We can help new teachers with this focus by making sure they

- Thoroughly understand the standards that are appropriate for their students.
- Communicate to students what is expected of them.

- Design learning experiences that will help students meet the standards.
- Assess students to see if they are meeting the standards.
- Adjust and reteach as needed to help each student learn what the standard requires.
- Communicate to parents which standards are being met and how their children are progressing in relation to the standards.

Teachers are challenged to create a rich learning environment when they focus on specific standards for learning. They have goals in mind for their students and they know how to determine whether students are meeting those goals. Their reflections are focused on what students are learning and how well they are learning.

> My biggest challenge has been in planning activities to teach to the standards. They [the standards] seem way beyond my kids' abilities.
>
> Third-year teacher

THE INTASC STANDARDS AND REFLECTIVE PRACTICE

The INTASC Standards call upon the teacher to be a "reflective practitioner who continually evaluates the effects of his/her choices and actions on others (students, parents, and other professionals in the learning community) and who actively seeks out opportunities to grow professionally" (Principle 9, INTASC, 1992).

Inherent in each principle is the assumption that teaching cannot be reduced to simple rules or recipes. Each standard is multifaceted and includes three key components that lend to rich, deep reflections about teaching: knowledge, dispositions, and performances.

Knowledge. Many forms of knowledge are important for teachers. Teachers need to know and understand the theoretical underpinning of what they do. They need to understand the content of what they teach. They need to be aware of a wide variety of strategies to use in classrooms and when each approach might be effective. They need to know how to recognize when their teaching is ineffective and be able to adjust accordingly. They need to know and understand their students and their cultures so that they can effectively connect their students with relevant learning opportunities. They are not satisfied that they ever know all there is to know about teaching, about their students, and about the subjects they teach.

The reflective piece is the crux of what we are doing because if you can help the new teacher really focus on the idea of reflection and self-criticism . . . that's what will eventually make that person . . . a better teacher. We're lifelong learners as teachers.

Support provider (mentor)
(Wing & Jinks, 2001, p. 39)

Dispositions. Teachers hold certain beliefs about and commitments toward students and learning. INTASC calls these "dispositions." Each INTASC principle includes a description of the dispositions that we expect teachers to bring to the classroom. For teachers to be reflective about their work, they need to value critical thinking, commit to reflection, be willing and open to receiving help, seek out new ideas, and fully embrace their responsibilities. Reflective teachers are committed in every sense of the word. They care about their students and strive to understand and meet their learning needs. Each INTASC principle includes a description of the dispositions that we expect teachers to bring to the classroom (see sample in Exhibit 6.3).

Performances. Teachers should understand and believe in what they do, but must also be able to exhibit practices that are effective and contribute to student learning. Teachers should be able put their knowledge to use and enact their beliefs in their interactions with their students in their own classrooms. They need to use their knowledge as a basis for their work. They need to draw upon what they know and the knowledge of others for new ideas and alternate approaches. In addition, teachers need to become a part of a professional learning community. The final part of each INTASC

Exhibit 6.3   Dispositions of the Reflective Practitioner

- The teacher values critical thinking and self-directed learning as habits of mind.
- The teacher is committed to reflection, assessment, and learning as an ongoing process.
- The teacher is willing to give and receive help.
- The teacher is committed to seeking out, developing, and continually refining practices that address the individual needs of students.
- The teacher recognizes his/her professional responsibility for engaging in and supporting appropriate professional practices for self and colleagues.

Source: INTASC (1992), p. 27.

standard deals with this ability to engage in these kinds of practices. Those who have used these standards to guide their induction programs have found them to be a rich resource for new teachers and their mentors. Teachers who use the standards as their guide to learning and growing find that the standards both stretch and enable them in their work. Their performance in the classroom with their students is the true test of their abilities.

THE CSTP AND REFLECTIVE PRACTICE

The California Standards (CSTP) were developed and validated in the context of diverse classrooms throughout California with extensive input from new teachers and their mentors. When these standards were developed, there was much discussion and debate among educators, followed by considerable field-testing and validation. What emerged as a consensus vision was not easily achieved—nor should it have been. Developing and codifying expectations for the profession is an important endeavor that demands our best thinking, research, expertise, and knowledge of practice.

The richness of the CSTP is the context they set for a deep, reflective examination of practice. New teachers are encouraged to examine their own practice in conversation with others. Each element of the six standards includes a set of reflective questions to stimulate this discussion. Each set of reflective questions is prefaced by the statement: As teachers develop, they may ask, "How do I . . ." or "Why do I . . ." Exhibit 6.4

Exhibit 6.4 Sample Reflective Questions from the California Standards for the Teaching Profession

---

Key Element: Establishing and communicating learning goals for all students.

As teachers develop, they may ask, "How do I . . ." or "Why do I . . ."

- Use subject matter standards from district, state, and other sources to guide how I establish learning goals for each student?
- Involve all students and families in establishing goals for learning?
- Review and revise learning goals with every student over time?
- Ensure that student learning goals reflect the key subject matter concepts, skills, and applications?
- Ensure that goals for learning are appropriate to my students' development, language acquisition, or other special needs?
- Ensure that my grading system reflects goals for student learning?
- Work with other educators to establish learning goals and assessment tools that promote student learning?

Source: CCTC and CDE (1997), p. 17.

provides a brief example of a set of reflective questions. The full CSTP document (www.ctc.ca.gov) contains more than 150 questions that can be used to guide these standards-based, reflective conversations.

Asking "how" and "why" questions in relation to standards encourages teachers and their mentors to probe for a rationale and example of ways that each standard might be met in that particular local context. These standards encourage teachers to learn more about their own students—their backgrounds, their cultures, and their lives. They encourage teachers to learn about and pursue a wide variety of strategies and practices in the classroom.

Like the INTASC standards, the CSTP standards encourage teachers to draw on their prior knowledge in their reflections. These standards and other standards like them call for careful attention to what educators themselves have defined as the important elements of teaching.

REFLECTIVE MENTORING

These standards require that teachers think about their profession in a nuanced way. They need a basis for understanding what further questions need to be asked, what and when to probe, and where to go to learn more. They use their knowledge to organize and reorganize learning experiences to engage their students. They recognize when students are not learning, determine why that might be so, and whether they can provide assistance.

> The program has been very relevant to what I am doing. The problems we have to write up are the problems that we are actually experiencing in the classroom. It helps me to think through those problems.
>
> First year teacher

Although many claim to be preparing teachers to be reflective in their work, not everyone agrees as to how best to foster and encourage a reflective approach to teaching. Most would agree that the groundwork for teacher reflection is laid in the preservice program. Valli (1997) categorized the approaches to teacher reflection as follows:

- *Technical reflection* focuses on specified domains of teaching techniques and skills and their application. Criteria for reflection are externally imposed and bounded by specific directions. Teachers reflect on how they are doing against those specified criteria. The content that teachers think about are the general teaching behaviors derived from research. Research is an important source of knowledge.

- *Reflection in action and reflection on action* focuses on having teachers look back on the experiences and events in the classroom and encouraging them to think critically about these occurrences and events. This approach emphasizes craft knowledge and personal experience.
- *Deliberative reflection* emphasizes decision making based on a variety of sources that may include research, experience, teacher advice, personal beliefs, and values. Teachers make decisions after gathering and analyzing evidence.
- *Personalistic reflection* focus on the teacher's personal growth and relational issues. Personal self-awareness and development is central in the approach. Teachers think about their own progress in light of their own background, training, and experience. They get know their students as persons—what motivates them and what is important in their lives.
- *Critical reflection* is based on concepts about beliefs about what is good or desirable. Political, social, and ethical questions about schooling are examined. The quality of teacher reflection is determined by the teacher's ability to apply ethical criteria to the goals and processes of schooling.

Valli argues against the adoption of one single, narrow approach to teacher reflection. She suggests the above approaches to reflection can be taught and used in combination with one another to help teachers develop full reflective capacity. Tools and techniques for reflection can be taught and encouraged in the induction program, but reflection itself is a mindset, a way of approaching one's life and work.

REFLECTIVE PRACTICE IN
THE INDUCTION YEARS

Reflection is quite natural in the context of the academic environment when preservice teachers are focused on reading, discussing, and reacting to ideas. This reflective stance encouraged in preservice does not always carry over into induction and actual classroom practice. Teachers often leave behind what they consider to be "just theory" when faced with the busy, stressful real-life world of classroom practice. They often fail to see the connections between what they have debated, discussed, and learned in the programs and their day-to-day worlds.

Teachers no longer have time to make journal entries, read, visit other classrooms, or problem-solve with their colleagues. No one is requiring them to present and defend their philosophies and ideas about best practice. No one is asking them to read and discuss research. Because new teachers are caught up with the task and responsibilities of teaching, they believe that they do not have time to engage in a careful and thoughtful examination of what they are doing and why they are doing it. Time to reflect becomes an impractical luxury.

Teachers who leave their preparation programs feeling that they are finished reflecting about their practice are most likely to let their work become routine and to discontinue their earlier reflective practices. Teachers who have no mentor or no peers with this orientation lack the colleagues who might stimulate further professional dialogue and reflection. The challenge is to extend teacher reflection beyond the walls of academia.

> Reflection? I just don't have time for that. I'm barely getting papers graded and lessons prepared for the next day.
>
> First-year teacher

Without guidance, new teachers do what seems expedient and "what works." Often this is learned by trial and error, or by picking up tips from the teacher next door, rather than in any systematic way.

However, induction programs are changing that attitude as educators attempt to develop a better bridge between preservice education and the initial years of practice. Mager (1992) describes this period as a time in which new teachers "continue to form and refine their images of themselves as teachers in terms of their competence, performance, and effectiveness" (p. 20). It is a time to extend and apply their prior learning, and to do some in a context where reflection can be enriched and informed by actual day-to-day practice.

Reflection will most likely to occur if it fostered in the context of the induction program and teachers are continued to be guided and supportive in reflective practice. They need time and opportunity to reflect. They need to reflect with others. They need discussion and dialogue about their emerging teaching practices, beliefs, and understandings.

Yet reflection during these intense, difficult times is challenging. New teachers often feel so overwhelmed with the task of day-to-day preparation and activities that they have little time to ponder what they are doing and what kind of impact they are having on students. They focus primarily on getting through the material, staying on schedule, and keeping the classroom under control. That is why "survival" is such an apt description of this phase of teaching.

A key role for the mentor and others who support the new teacher is to guide and support the practice of reflection. The mentor helps the new teacher survive, but cannot stop providing support when survival needs have been met. We want and need so much more from our teachers—from all of our teachers, beginning as well as the more experienced. Our students deserve to be taught by teachers who have higher aspirations for themselves, by those who aspire to be successful, reflective practitioners that are guided by standards of practice.

SOME CAUTIONS ABOUT REFLECTIVE PRACTICE

Some cautions about reflective practice should be noted. There is a danger that reflection can turn inward and therefore be limited by one's own knowledge, understanding, and worldview. When teachers are encouraged to simply follow their own intuition and inner voice, their reflections tend to become narrow and individualistic (Valli, 1997). If no new ideas, information, or understandings are introduced into the reflective process, teacher reflection may simply validate biases, stereotypes, false assumptions, or inaccuracies.

An example of this is the teacher who teaches a lesson through an activity that seems to "work." When probed about this, the teacher may reply that, upon reflection, the activity engaged students. The teacher believes that students seemed to understand what they were doing. However, this teacher has not reflected upon anything but the obvious, which is student engagement.

This teacher needs to probe deeper into the value of that learning activity. What was to be accomplished? How will she know that the learning goals have been met? Did all students or just some of them meet these goals? What information can she gather to support her feeling that the activity was successful?

Reflective practice may be hampered by a teacher's inability to identify students' specific needs. Beginning teachers are often not yet adept at posing these deeper questions. They need further guidance and mentoring to help them pose the right questions and reach beyond the obvious in their reflections. Like their own students, they don't know what to ask, what to examine, and what to probe.

Feiman-Nemser (2001) indicates that "problem construction" is challenging for the novice. She shares an example of how management is identified as the pressing problem for the novice, yet the real problem may have more to do with curriculum and instruction, and an inability to engage diverse learners in meaningful and challenging tasks.

Mentor: I was wondering about your special needs students and if there would be anything you might do to differentiate the instruction for some students to make this a more successful lesson for them?

New Teacher: That's actually, that's probably one question that I did not come up with, but I had it in the back of my mind that I wanted to ask you how I could help those students. I would like some guidance from you on that one. I'm finding it a challenge right now and I would like some guidance from you.

Achinstein and Barrett (2003), p. 30.

In studying the transcripts of conversations between new teachers and mentor, Achinstein and Barrett (2003) found that mentors played a significant role in helping new teachers reframe or better name and understand their own problems. They found that reframing by a mentor offers the novice a repertoire of ways to diagnose problems and alternative approaches to managing challenges. Mentors can share their more expert schemata and ways of seeing a problem.

There is a danger in that by trying to get teachers to be reflective, we become overly prescriptive about what they are to reflect upon and how they are to go about it. Another danger is in the structuring of reflection activities and insisting that teachers follow specific formats for reflective practice as if there is only one proper way to reflect. Fendler (2003) cautions that

> When teacher education researchers provide elaborate programs for teaching teachers to be reflective practitioners, the implicit assumption is that teachers are not reflective unless they practice the specific techniques promoted by the researchers. It is ironic that rhetoric about reflective practitioners focuses on empowering teachers, but the requirements of learning to be reflective are based on the assumption that teachers are incapable of reflection without direction from expert authorities. (p. 23)

There is a balance to be found in guiding teachers to reflective practice that they generate from their own experience but that also is able to advance and extend their thinking and improve their practice. We need to aim for that balance in teacher-preparation and induction programs. We do that by helping them see beyond their own narrow interpretations and by structuring opportunities for reflection in community with others.

Reflection can be a bridge from preservice to induction. It brings the knowledge of preservice forward to be tried, tested, modified, and lived out in practice.

REFLECTION IN COMMUNITY

Learning to teach, whether it occurs in a traditional preservice program or in one of the many alternative-route programs that have emerged, is done with others. Prospective teachers learn and study with others, work on group projects and activities, debate and discuss ideas, and observe others teach. Thus, community is built into the preparation program. There are many individuals who help to expand the scope of the preservice teacher's thinking. Preservice teachers reflect with one another in their classes and in their field experience. They reflect with their instructors and supervisors and get feedback from them on a regular basis.

Until we became intentional about the induction experience, the opportunities for collegial dialogue and discussion among new teachers and their colleagues was rare. New teachers operated in their own classrooms with little interaction with other teachers. Perhaps they had a visit from the principal once or twice during the year. Perhaps they had a colleague who offered occasional tips and advice, but rarely had deep and thoughtful conversations about teaching practice and student achievement.

Induction programs that provide mentoring and other interactive experiences among colleges makes it possible for that reflection in community to continue beyond initial preparation into the early years. New teachers are visited frequently by their mentors, observe others' teaching, and discuss educational issues and ideas with their colleagues. Their teaching is observed on a regular basis and they get feedback about what they are doing. Reflection in community is a key aspect of the well-designed induction experience.

TOOLS TO ENHANCE REFLECTION

A number of tools are used to help teachers develop reflective habits in preservice and induction years. Some of the more commonly used approaches are described here.

Journals. Teachers keep track of their own experiences in learning to teach in a journal. Journals may be kept in a booklet or in electronic format. Entries are made on a regular basis and students use this to reflect back on their planning for a lesson, how it was taught, and what students learned. They are often asked to reflect on what they could have done differently, or how they will follow up on the lesson. They may also describe how their experience with their students relates to something they have learned. They pose questions for further clarification. Sometimes the journal is shared with others—it may be a faculty member, a mentor, or a colleague. If the journal is interactive, the other persons will pose questions, probe, and mention other things to consider in response to the teacher's entries.

Life histories or narrative. Autobiographical writing is a way for individuals to investigate and record the ways in which their personal experiences shape and influences their thinking about teaching. The writer seeks to probe deeply held perceptions, assumptions, and beliefs. Self-awareness becomes a route to fuller understanding of others and their experiences. Prospective and practicing teachers explore, in writing, their own lives and professional practices through narrative. Teacher narratives that are shared often help us all to discuss and understand the complexities of classroom practice.

Cases. Cases are rich, detailed descriptions of concrete teaching episodes (Shulman, 1986). They usually focus on specific events or classroom experiences in the classroom context. Embedded in the case descriptions are key elements of theoretical principles that can be discussed and used to enlighten practice. Cases are often used to illustrate conflicts or problems that they teacher would encounter. Teachers often study, analyze, and discuss cases as a way to learn more about the complexities and nuances of practices. They may also write cases themselves as a way of reflecting on and sharing their experiences with others.

Action Research. Action research is a form of systematic inquiry into practice in order to more fully understand and improve that practice. Kemmis and McTaggart (1988) describe the process as one that requires an individual to plan, act, observe, and reflect. Teachers conduct action research in their own classrooms in order to better understand their students and the context for teaching and learning. They learn how to gather information to help them make sound, informed decisions. They reflect individually and with others on the information they have gathered. Finally, they make decisions about their future actions and direction based on what they have learned.

Structured Observations. Observations of teaching help to provide information about what is happening in the classroom. Teachers may observe or be observed by others. If that observer has a purpose or purposes in mind during the visit, the observation will be structured around that purpose. For example, a teacher may observe another to see how that teacher individualizes assignments for students of varying ability levels. A supervisor may observe a student teacher to see how that individual is progressing toward meeting the standards or expectations for the student teaching experience. A mentor may observe because the new teacher has asked for specific help with classroom management. Structured observations provide information to be used in follow up discussions about the issue or problem at hand.

Collegial Group Discussions. When students are preparing to teach, they need opportunities to explore, question, discuss, and debate ideas with others. They share what they are learning and critique the work of their colleagues. They reflect with other on their own strengths and weaknesses and develop plans to improve. This group interaction needs to be built into preservice as well as the induction years.

Reflective Problem Solving. Thompson and Zeuli (1999) speak of "reflective problem solving," referring to "individual or collaborative efforts to resolve some puzzle or conflict between observed and actual practice, interaction with students, or encounter with subject matter" (p. 363).

A variation on this approach is "problem-based learning," or problem solving that is situated in the real world of practice. In working through real or constructed problems, teachers learn to draw upon many ideas and resources. They learn to be thoughtful in approaching their work and to consider the complexity of the context. As they investigate alternative solutions, they learn more about themselves, their students, and how to handle a similar issue in the future.

WHERE DOES STANDARDS-BASED REFLECTION LEAD?

Reflective teachers who are guided by standards that present a vision of expertise continue to learn, grow, and develop teaching expertise throughout their careers. For reflective practitioners, there is always more to learn, new ideas to think about, and room for improvement. Each colleague becomes a source of information, ideas, and resources. Each student is a new challenge, a new mind to be shaped and developed. Each school year presents new opportunities to make a difference in student lives and student learning.

Reflective teachers learn in and from their practice. Ball and Cohen (1999) note that a "stance of inquiry" is central to the role of teaching, distinguishing between simply becoming experienced and actually learning from experience and improving one's practice. Reflective teachers learn how to investigate what students are doing and thinking, and how instruction has been understood and embraced as classes unfold. Reflective practitioners are able to size up a situation from moment to moment, use their knowledge to improve their practice, and operate experimentally in response to students and situations.

Reflective practitioners know that strategies and approaches that appear to work for one student or group of students may not work for another. They enthusiastically take on new challenges, adapt generic texts and teaching materials to their students' needs, share ideas with colleagues, and teach their students to be reflective learners.

Reflective practitioners operate most effectively as a member of a reflective professional community. As Little (1999) asserts, "teacher learning arises out of close involvement with students and their work, shared responsibility for student progress, . . . access to the expertise of colleagues inside and outside of the school, . . . feedback on one's own work, and an overall ethos in which teacher learning is valued" (p. 233).

It is difficult to sustain reflective practice in an environment that does not support or value reflection. A reflective practitioner needs colleagues that share this perspective and will work with one another to improve practice for all teachers and more importantly, learning for all students. Kruse, Louis, and Bryk (1995) describe the five core characteristics of such a professional community as follows:

Shared Norms and Values. A set of shared beliefs about institutional purposes, practices, and desired behavior that are discussed, made explicit, and serve as a basis for schoolwide decision making.

Reflective Dialogue. Conversations that hold practice, pedagogy, and student learning under scrutiny.

Deprivatization of Practice. Teachers within professional communities practice their craft openly, sharing and trading off the roles of mentor, advisor, or specialist when providing aid and assistance to peers.

Collective Focus on Student Learning. Sustained attention to students at the core of schoolwide professional community. Teachers' beliefs and values wholeheartedly support notions of children as academically capable.

Collaboration. Genuine collaboration that extends beyond cooperation or collegiality is a generalized attribute of the schoolwide professional community. Colleagues across grade level, work groups, and content areas learn from one another. (pp. 28–34)

Teachers are inducted into a particular community, in a particular setting, working with a particular group of students. That school community needs to be an integral part of the collegiality and collaboration that surrounds beginning teaching—teaching that is marked by reflection and collaboration.

This vision of the reflective practitioner calls for induction into a standards-based profession that nurtures and develops reflective practice in its members. It argues for mentoring and support in a collegial environment that values, supports, and facilitates the growth of its membership. It is an induction into a professional community.

IMPLICATIONS FOR PRACTICE

The main points of this chapter and their implications for practice can be summarized as follows:

1. Induction plans should be guided by professional standards for teachers and learning outcomes or standards for students.

2. Reflective teaching is characterized by deep, careful thought and careful examination of practice. Reflective teachers are decision makers, problem posers, and problem solvers.

3. Standards provide a common set of expectations and a common language for talking about excellence in teaching. They provide an impetus toward reflective practice and a basis for reflection.

4. The INTASC Standards and the California Standards for the Teaching Profession serve as examples of standards to guide reflective practice.

5. Teachers will be held accountable for student learning and for helping their students meet the standards that have been established for student learning in their states and in their schools. We can help new teachers by making sure they
   • Thoroughly understand the standards appropriate for their students.
   • Communicate to students what is expected of them.
   • Design learning experiences that will help students meet the standards.
   • Assess students to see if they are meeting the standards.
   • Adjust and reteach as needed to help each child learn what the standard requires.
   • Communicate to parents which standards are being met and how their students are progressing in relation to the standards.

6. Types of reflective practice include technical reflection; reflection in action and reflection on action; deliberative reflection; personalistic reflection; and critical reflection. All can be taught and used effectively in the induction program.

7. Reflective practice in the induction years can help build a bridge from preservice to induction.

8. Mentors can help new teachers identify their needs and name their problems in a reflective conversation.

9. Reflection in community is often richer than that done in isolation.

10. Tools used to facilitate reflection include journals, life history or narrative, cases, action research, structured observations, collegial group discussions, and reflective problem solving.

11. Reflective practice is encouraged in a community that fosters shared norms and values, reflective dialogue, deprivatization of practice, a collective focus on student learning, and collaboration.

FOR FURTHER READING

Benson, B. P. (2003). *How to meet standards, motivate, students, and still enjoy teaching.* Thousand Oaks, CA: Corwin.
This book focuses on four practices that combine all the components necessary to meet the demands of standards-based instruction while also improving student learning by
   • Creating a community of learners through self-directed learning, interactive classrooms, and student cooperation.

- Making reflection a routine part of the classroom for both teachers and students.
- Teaching content and process.
- Using more authentic student assessment methods.

Bray, J. N., Lee, J., Smith, L. L., & Yorks, L. (2000). *Collaborative inquiry in practice: Action, reflection, and making meaning.* Thousand Oaks, CA: Sage.
The book is a guide for people interested in pursuing an imaginative and holistic approach to human inquiry. The reader is guided step-by-step through the theory and practice of collaborative inquiry. The author discusses the relationship of collaborative inquiry with other action-oriented methods of inquiry and explains the conduct of collaborative inquiry, from forming a group to constructing knowledge. The authors demonstrate how effective collaborative inquiry demystifies research and makes learning more accessible. The guidance provided is equally relevant to professional and academic settings.

Darling-Hammond, L. (1997). *The right to learn: A blueprint for creating schools that work.* San Francisco: Jossey-Bass.
This book describes what needs to make our schools both learner centered and learning centered. The author argues for an approach to education policy that is designed to build the capacity of educators to be responsible for student learning and to be responsive to student and community needs. She emphasizes that well-defined standards for teachers and students should not standardize, but should be used to build that capacity. She documents the uneven distribution of qualified teachers and argues for providing equal opportunity to learn for all students.

Eby, J. W., Herrell, A. L., Hicks, J., & Hicks, J. L. (2001*). Reflective planning, teaching and evaluation: K–12,* 3rd ed. Englewood Cliffs, NJ: Prentice Hall.
The authors describe how reflective teachers think about and plan for their work with students. Among the areas covered are diagnosis of student needs; motivational techniques; cooperative learning; daily and long-range planning strategies; making the environment safe for children; the integration of computer technology into the classroom; developing self-esteem; and evaluation of student progress. They also provide specific strategies for meeting the needs of students with cultural, linguistic and learning differences.

Henderson, J. G. (1992). *Reflective teaching: Becoming an inquiring educator.* New York: Macmillan.
The author begins with a description of the model of reflective teaching presented in this book, which includes an ethic of caring, a constructivist approach to teaching, and artistic problem solving. The book emphasizes processes of inquiry and reflection grounded in a knowledge base about teaching, learning, and curriculum. Cases of teaching are presented for discussion and analysis in this book that is theoretical grounded but practical in application.

Schmuck, R. A. (1997). *Practical action research for change.* Arlington Heights, IL: Skylight Training and Publishing.
This book shows how reflective practice and action research can work together to serve as a source for developing professionalism team problem-solving skills and

democratic relationships in school communities. It is a step-by-step guide for practitioners who want to conduct action research, illustrated with examples. Practical tips for collecting data, for individual and group reflection, and for effectively implementing action research are included.

Schön, D. A. (1987). *Educating the reflective practitioner: Toward a new design for teaching and learning in the professions.* San Francisco: Jossey-Bass.
This seminal work on the reflective practitioner argues that the practice of the professions are rarely straightforward and clear. Skillful practice often depends less on factual knowledge but on the ability to reflect before taking action. The author argues for professional education that would enlarge the ability of practitioners for "reflection in action" and for problem solving throughout the individual's career. He shows how professional schools can use this approach to prepare students to handle the complex and unpredictable problems of actual practice.

Taggart, G. L., & Wilson, A. P. (1998). *Promoting reflective thinking in teachers: 44 Action strategies.* Thousand Oaks, CA: Corwin.
This book is designed to help teacher educators and staff developers facilitate reflective practice in teachers. Strategies for reflective practice are presented at three levels: technical, contextual, and dialectical. As the title indicates, practical action strategies are presented. Each chapter begins with objectives to help the facilitator in presenting thinking models, assessments, and strategies. Each strategy includes a complete explanation along with reflective activities and questions to make implementation easy.

York-Barr, J., Sommers, W. A., Ghere, G. S., & Montie, J. (2001). *Reflective practice to improve schools: An action guide for educators.* Thousand Oaks, CA: Corwin.
The authors recognize that educators need real opportunities to continuously and meaningfully reflect on their practice—by themselves and with their colleagues—to create schools in which both students and adults continually learn. The book includes
- A framework and strategies for reflective thinking and acting.
- Essential considerations for designing and developing reflective practices.
- Examples of reflective practice at the individual level, between partners, in small groups, and schoolwide.
- Reflective activities to guide individuals and collaborators toward applied strategies.

Udelhofen, S., & Larson, K. (2003). *The mentoring year: A step-by-step program for professional development.* Thousand Oaks, CA: Corwin.
This approach to mentoring is grounded in nationally developed standards for the teaching profession. The authors show how to encourage a learning community, team building approach to mentor for success, student achievement, and teacher retention. Many rubrics for measuring growth of the new teacher toward best practice are included.

7

Teacher Assessment

T eachers are assessed in a variety of ways at various points in their careers. They are assessed for formative and summative purposes. Induction programs may include assessments that serve both purposes. This chapter discusses the role that standards-driven assessment plays in the induction program. It shows how assessments of teaching can be used to foster reflective practice in developing teachers.

STANDARDS-DRIVEN ASSESSMENT

Beginning teachers want to know how they are doing and can benefit from thoughtful feedback about their practice. If they are struggling, they want help with specific problems or concerns. Sometimes they know they need help, but cannot identify the help they need or the questions to ask. Yet teachers often do not receive the feedback they want or need, or they get feedback that is too vague to be useful.

> I guess I am doing OK. My mentor did come and observe my teaching. But he didn't give me much feedback—many suggestions. I would like to have specific suggestions about what I can do better.
>
> Second-year teacher

Chapter 6 presented a discussion of the role of professional standards in guiding the support of new teachers toward thoughtful, reflective practice. Well-developed standards can give new teachers and their mentors a common set of understandings about what constitutes best practice.

This guidance is enriched if it is informed by thorough assessments of teacher performance. Well-designed, standards-driven assessments of teaching performance help to inform new teachers and their mentors about how the new teachers are doing. Such assessments can point out what teachers know, understand, and do well, as well as target areas for improvement. They can encourage expansion of knowledge, skills, and thoughtful practice.

Assessments grounded in agreed upon teaching expectations provide information about how teachers are progressing along the dimensions specified in the standards.

The Board's work [National Board for Professional Teaching Standards] illustrates how standards of knowledge can be applied to open-end, contextualized representations of teaching without resorting to simplistic checklists. By looking at similar tasks about which evidence is collected and presented in a structured manner, it is possible to evaluate candidates against common standards.

Darling-Hammond, Wise, & Klein (1999), p. 84.

Porter, Youngs, and Odden (2001) describe three purposes of teacher assessment:

1. To control the movement of teachers into and out of positions at different stages of their careers.

2. To influence the performance and professional growth of teachers in particular positions.

3. To represent professional consensus about the knowledge and skills that teachers must have to engage in responsible practice. (p. 259)

These three purposes are relevant to the assessments that have been developed as a part of induction systems. In some places, assessments conducted in the induction period determine who receives the credential. In other places, the assessments are designed to give specific feedback to new teachers about their development and to guide them to the appropriate professional development opportunities, or, in some cases, to provide counsel that they may not be well suited for teaching. The assessments used in induction have typically been designed around a professional consensus about good practice, and thus become a springboard for discussions and guidance toward that vision, such as the vision described in the examples of the Interstate New Teacher Assessment and Support Consortium (INTASC) and California standards.

What is missing in Porter's list is the ultimate purpose of teacher assessment: to improve student learning. Teachers are assessed so that they can improve their ability to reach and serve students. The assessment of teachers and the assessment of student progress are integrally linked. Teachers cannot be successful if their students do not succeed or do not show progress in meeting the standards set for them.

The new systems of teacher assessment in induction programs are often performance-based; that is, they are designed to measure the complexity of teaching in the classroom context. These assessments are more than paper-and-pencil tests; they rely on artifacts and examples of teaching experience in the classroom. Performance-based approaches usually take a holistic approach to examining teaching, examining not only what a teacher does in the teaching act, but how the teacher thinks about, plans, and analyzes the teaching and the student learning that occurs. These assessments also require that teacher and the assessors consider the context in which the teacher works.

> *Performance-Based Assessments: Assessments designed to measure teaching performance in authentic ways by using artifacts and examples of what teachers do in the classroom and evidence of how they think about, plan for, and evaluate their work and the work of their students.*

This chapter deals with teacher assessments and the role they play in induction programs. Although the terms *assessment* and *evaluation* are often used interchangeably, an important distinction is made here. Assessments refer to procedures, instruments, and protocols used to collect information about teacher performance. Evaluation refers to the purposes for which data and information are gathered. Assessment information may be used for evaluative purposes, but it may be used for other nonevaluative purposes as well. Assessments may guide discussions of practice that are not a part of the formal evaluation of the teacher's performance.

> *Assessments of Teaching: Procedures, instruments, and protocols used to collect information about teacher performance.*
>
> *Teaching Evaluations: Gathering information about teaching knowledge and practice in order to make judgments about teacher performance.*

INDUCTION ASSESSMENTS IN CONTEXT

The assessments of beginning teachers during an induction period should be considered in light of the range of assessments that are conducted of teachers during various points in their careers. While the requirements for formal evaluative assessments vary considerably by state, some typical patterns can be found across the country. As state and national policy makers demand more accountability, there has been a heightened interest in formal evaluative assessments of teaching.

Assessments of teaching potential and ability begins early in teachers' careers, before they begin to teach. Prospective teachers are assessed in various ways before they are admitted to teacher preparation programs. If it is required in their state, they may be tested on their basic skills (i.e., reading, math, and writing), general knowledge, or content knowledge. Most preparation programs used multiple methods to assess candidates at entry. Grade point average is one measure of overall academic competence. Most programs supplement this measure with information gleaned from interviews, writing samples, and evidence of past experiences working with young people.

Once they are admitted to the preparation program, assessments are designed to measure the teacher candidate's progress in meeting the standards established by their university or alternative program sponsor. These programs use a variety of strategies and devise a number of checkpoints to measure progress along the way. Most universities have established points at which, if the candidate is not meeting expectations, they are not allowed to continue in the program. Typically, most students will exit if they are not meeting academic requirements of if they fail to demonstrate satisfactory performance in their clinical teaching experience.

Checkpoints or benchmarks established along the way may be a part of the state requirements for earning a credential, such as a test of basic skills, assessments of pedagogy, knowledge, content, or performance. Universities also include evidence of their own choosing that show appropriate progress toward meeting the standards set forth by the program. This evidence may include such things as work samples, evaluations of clinical experiences, portfolio evidence, and course grades. Many programs have or are developing an exit assessment that is administered before a candidate can be recommended for a credential. This assessment can be either a locally designed assessment or one that has been developed at the state level or by a national testing company. Exit assessments may be performance-based or they may be paper and pencil tests. Recent federal legislation is reshaping this exit experience, as new federal requirements push for a more standardized way of measuring the ability to assess subject matter competence.

The implications for induction are that teachers are accustomed to being assessed throughout their preparation. It is logical to assume that they will continue to be assessed as they move into that formative induction period.

ASSESSMENTS IN INDUCTION

At the present time, teachers who enter classrooms have access to an induction program in at least twenty-eight states. In at least twenty of these states, there is a required assessment component associated with the induction activities (National Association of State Directors of Teacher Education and Certification, 2002). In some cases, the assessments are used to make a decision about whether or not to award an advanced-level credential. In other states, the assessments are used in a formative sense, shaping the support strategies and professional development that is provided. Examples of the former are Connecticut, Indiana, and Ohio; examples of the latter are Alabama and California.

During or at the end of the induction period, or perhaps soon after, most teachers are subject to being evaluated for tenure in their district. The assessments employed in this evaluation may or may not correspond to the assessments that are used to determine if the person is awarded a license to teach. Evaluations for tenure are usually conducted by the teacher's supervisor, and may or may not be driven by statewide standards and criteria.

The teacher may meet the requirements established for the state assessment and is awarded a teaching credential, but the employing district decides not to tenure that teacher. This teacher will still receive a credential, and is then free to seek another teaching position within that state. Teachers who fail the licensure assessment cannot hold a valid credential and may not continue to teach. However, in some states, failed assessments may be repeated, and assistance will be given for a limited amount of time to help teachers be able to perform at an appropriate level. In such cases, induction activities will be extended to provide such assistance.

ONGOING EVALUATION OF TEACHING

Teachers are subject to ongoing evaluations of their performance over the course of their careers. The principal or assistant principal typically conduct these evaluations using specified criteria. Appropriate professional growth plans based on these ongoing evaluations may be devised. In many states, peer assistance programs offer help to teachers who are in need of assistance at various stages of their careers. Increasingly, teaching standards are shaping these evaluations as well.

> My mentor helped me get ready for the Stull [designation for formal evaluation by the principal]. He did a practice run with me and everything. He gave me some good pointers too. He told me what she (the principal) would be looking for. When the principal came, I was ready.
>
> Second-year teacher

Another more recent point of assessment is for experienced teachers who wish to become nationally board certified. The National Board for Professional Teaching Standards was created in 1987 as the result of a report issued by the Carnegie Forum on Education and the Economy. The report called for the founding of a professional body to establish high standards for teachers and to certify those who meet them. The purpose of the board is to certify teachers who meet high standards and to recognize excellence in teaching. The assessments are performance-based, and include teaching portfolios, student work samples, videotapes, and a series of written exercises. Participation in the assessments developed by the National Board is purely voluntary, but many states and districts provide monetary and other incentives for those who are able to become nationally board certified (National Board for Professional Teaching Standards, www.nbpts.org).

FORMATIVE AND SUMMATIVE ASSESSMENTS

Assessment can be used in a formative way or for summative purposes. Scriven (1967) made the distinction between the formative role of evaluation feedback when used internally to make program improvement and the summative role when used by outsiders to make final decisions about funding or adoption of a program.

> She was worried about me observing her. But then, when she realized that we were just going to use this for more reflection back into the lesson, it really started to boost her confidence.
>
> Support provider (Mentor)
> (Wing & Jinks, 2001, p. 46)

The principles can be applied to evaluations of teaching performance. The goal of formative evaluation is to identify teachers' strengths and weaknesses and plan for appropriate professional development activities. Summative evaluation provides a basis for administrative decisions involving licensing, hiring, promotion, tenure, and assignments. Both serve important functions.

Teachers may be assessed for both formative and summative purposes during their induction years. Formative assessments give feedback to mentors and others who provide support for new teachers. Formative assessments are not used in an evaluative sense or to make decisions about retention, tenure, or promotion. They are designed to provide feedback to new teachers and their mentors so that they can make appropriate plans for professional development. Summative assessments are employed at key decision points and provide information about credentialing, tenure, retention, or promotion.

These distinctions are not always so clear. In many cases, assessments are intended to serve both formative and summative purposes. Information may be shared with teachers and their mentors for purposes of planning support services, but may also be used at some point in an evaluative way.

> *Formative Assessments: Measures of teaching performance employed to provide feedback to teachers so that they can improve their practice.*
>
> *Summative Assessments: Measures of teaching performance employed at key decision points and provide information about credentialing, tenure, retention, or promotion.*

ASSESSMENT APPROACHES

There are a variety of ways to assess teacher knowledge and performance. Some of the more commonly used approaches to testing teacher knowledge are through the multiple-choice exams or open-ended, constructed-response items that require teachers to write about a particular issue or topic.

The newer forms of assessment are designed to measure teaching performance in more complex, authentic ways by using artifacts and examples of what teachers do in the classroom and evidence of how they think about, plan for, and evaluate their work and the work of their students.

The assessments of teaching described here range from simple to complex, following a continuum suggested by Tushnet, Briggs, Elliot, Esch, Haviland, Humphrey, et al. (2002). These researchers suggest, as do most others familiar with assessments of teaching, that "given the limitations of any single approach to assessing teacher knowledge and skills, some type of integrated system is needed" (p. 165).

Closed-End or Multiple-Choice Tests. Multiple-choice items are traditionally used in tests of teaching or content knowledge because they offer the ability to sample across a wide number of domains. They are easy to administer and score, and are relatively inexpensive. Well-crafted items can measure knowledge as well as the teacher's ability to analyze and synthesize information. They have, however, been widely criticized for their inability to measure the complexity of teaching in context.

Student Test Score Gains. Student test scores are increasingly being advocated as a way to measure the performance of the school as a whole or, in some cases, individual teachers. The idea of linking student test score gains to the performance of the individual is appealing to many who argue that teachers should be held accountable for the measurable results in their students. Others argue that student gains are influenced by many factors and that extend beyond the influence of what the teacher does in the classroom.

Student Surveys. Feedback from students is considered a fairly reliable indicator of teacher performance, especially if the surveys are administered at multiple points in time. They are probably most appropriate for older students. However, students may respond to these items based on other characteristics than those being measured.

Teacher Surveys. Surveys have the advantage of enabling us to collect large amounts of data very efficiently. Surveys are used to gather information about beliefs and self-reports of practice. They can be administered at multiple points in time, giving us the ability to measure changes over time.

Portfolio Assessment. A portfolio is a collection of teaching materials, lesson plans, student work, and other artifacts that represent the teacher's work. It may also include a video of the teacher in the classroom with students. It usually includes teacher reflections about the entries and artifacts collected. The collection may be in paper format, in a notebook, or it may be electronically based. The evidence in the assessment portfolio is collected to demonstrate how teachers are meeting particular standards. Using a rubric, assessors judge the quality of the evidence based on predetermined criteria. Because teachers themselves select evidence of the best work over time, portfolio evidence gives a fuller picture of teaching than some of the other measures. However, it is time-consuming to construct and to review.

Teacher Self-Reports. These are usually in the form of a log of activities or teacher diary. Teachers record events and their reflections about particular aspects of their work that may be examined and analyzed by others. Self-reports are most useful in obtaining records of such things as number and duration of lessons taught, materials and procedures used, and information about students. They have limited ability to measure teacher knowledge and skills.

Teacher Interviews. Interviews of teachers provide information about the knowledge and about teaching plans. Interviews are most often used in combination with other approaches. For example, teachers may be interviewed before and after a classroom observation to provide a fuller context for the observer.

Classroom Observations. Direct classroom observations are another way to assess the teacher's work. Observations rely on trained observers who make judgments about how well certain teaching abilities are demonstrated. Observers or evaluators are trained to use a specific instrument or protocol so that judgments rendered will be valid and reliable. The classroom observation measures what is seen at a particular time in a given setting. They are relatively costly to use in any reliable way, because of the training involved and the time spent observing.

Open-Ended Tests. Written tests usually consist of multiple-choice items and/or open-ended questions or prompts to which the teacher responds. Open-ended items call for a constructed response, which is more time-consuming to read and score. A rubric is developed for scoring purposes, and those who are scoring the items are trained to apply the rubric in a consistent manner. The advantage of the constructed response item is that teachers can provide in-depth responses to questions or situations.

Directed Activities. Directed activities are similar to open-ended test items. Teachers respond to a prompt or analyze an aspect of teaching that is directed in the guidelines for the assessment activity. This approach is often used in portfolio construction or at a specific location such as an assessment center.

Simulation Exercises. Simulations may be tasks to which teachers respond instructional problems they are asked to solve. The most common simulations are presented in written form or as in-basket activities. However, newer forms of simulations are computer based. Assessors are able to controlling and standardize the activity (the tasks, the students, the setting, etc.) across all teachers, permitting an evaluation of a specific set of skills.

In addition to arraying these assessment approaches from simple to complex, Tushnet et al. (2002) also make the distinction between assessment that is proximate, or close to the actual act of teaching and those that are distal, or most distant from actual teaching. Classroom observations fall into the proximate category, followed by portfolios, teacher surveys, teacher self-reports. Teacher interviews, student test scores, student surveys, closed ended tests, open-ended tests, simulations, and directed activities are classified as most distal. Those approaches that are the most distant from actual classroom practice are the most likely to present an artificial view of what is actually happening in the classroom. Those that are too simplistic measure only a very narrow concept of what teaching is about.

Those planning to include assessments that will inform practice in the induction period have a rich array of approaches from which to select.

Many assessment experts (Darling-Hammond, 2001; Porter et al., 2001) advocate that using a variety of approaches at multiple points in time gives us a fuller picture of the teacher's knowledge, ability, and impact on students.

EXAMPLES OF PERFORMANCE-BASED ASSESSMENTS IN PRACTICE

In Chapter 6, two early standards development activities were discussed. The development of both the INTASC and the California standards was accompanied by work on new forms of assessments that might help measure attainment of these standards. Many states have used or modified the INTASC assessments for their own induction activities. Others have developed their own forms of assessments. In some places, these assessments are used only in a formative way. In others, assessments serve both formative and summative assessment purposes. In still others, there is only a summative use of assessment data.

Induction programs are strengthened by the use of assessments for formative purposes. Teachers receive specific feedback about how they are progressing toward the established standards. If the performance-based assessments measure such progress, teachers and their mentors can discuss that assessment information to develop goals and plans for that new teacher's professional development during that crucial induction phase.

The assessment systems described in this chapter were designed to provide this meaningful feedback to the developing teacher. Although both assessment systems are performance-based and were designed to measure the complexity of teaching in the context of the classroom, there are some key differences in the design and use of these assessments. A primary difference is in their ultimate use. The INTASC assessments are designed to foster critical examination and ongoing reflection of teaching practice, as well as to make a summative decision about teacher licensing. The California system is designed for formative purposes only. Other differences can be noted in the following sections of this chapter. Both are presented as examples of the new approach to developing performance-based assessments that are shaping rich, reflective discussions among teachers about their practice.

INTASC ASSESSMENTS

The INTASC standards are assessments that are grounded in disciplinary areas. The content-specific standards were drawn from the core standards, but focus on appropriate ways of presenting that specific subject matter to students.

The assessments are portfolio-based. Teachers submit a collection of evidence of their practice to a panel to be evaluated and scored. The kind of evidence submitted is best illustrated by an examination of one of the first portfolio assessments developed for INTASC, the math assessment. For the INTASC math assessment, teachers submit six portfolio entries that are integrated around an instructional unit. The content of the entries is summarized below as an example of subject specific assessment.

For the first task, teachers provide a description of the teaching context, including information about the community in which their school is located, status and gender distribution of the students, level of students (middle or high school), whether they teach in a public or private school, and their access to technology. They also describe their school, the class they have selected for assessment, and the three students on which they will focus in the assessment tasks.

For the second entry, teachers complete detailed lesson plans that include the mathematics, tasks, discourse, environment, and analysis that occurs in this series of lessons. They also outline their objectives for student learning and describe the mathematical concepts that unify the lessons. They also include any modifications they will make for the three students they have selected.

The third and fourth entries require that the teacher videotape two lessons and include twenty to thirty minutes of each lesson. Videotapes are expected to include the introduction and development of a mathematical concept, whole-group and non–whole-group instruction, and students' engagement in problem solving. The videotape is accompanied by commentary, samples of student work, and an analysis of the lesson.

The fifth entry describes the assessments used and an analysis of student learning. Again, information specific to the three selected students is included. For the final entry, teachers assess the collection of work in their portfolios and describe how it will be used for their own professional growth (INTASC, 1995a).

Teachers are encouraged to work with a mentor in preparing their portfolios. As they do so, they engage in conversations about what evidence they are including and why they selected that particular piece of evidence. This collaborative conversation encourages collegial practices and reflection on what constitutes best practice. This requires a continual revisiting of the standards that guide and shape not only the collecting of evidence, but the analysis of that evidence. Teachers focus on the standards for their level or disciplinary areas, as well as the practices outlined in the Core Standards.

The approach to evaluating these portfolios is similar to the one used by the National Board for Professional Teaching. Two trained assessors evaluate the evidence submitted and assign a rating on each element. Raters are required to compare and integrate evidence from multiple parts of the portfolio to arrive at a judgment. Readers then use their own analysis to compare and discuss the rating with the other reader to arrive at agreement. States using this assessment for licensure purposes (e.g., Connecticut) decide what the cut scores will be and determine if there will be a resubmission process for those who fail.

Moss, Schutz, and Collins (1998) describe this as "an integrative approach" and indicate that

> this kind of work has the potential to assist the community of teachers and teacher educators in developing and critically evaluating empirically based performance standards for beginning teachers through a process that is meaningful and accessible to all members of the educational community. Unlike conventional practices of standard setting, where judgments about teaching are based on decontextualized pieces of information statistically combined to determine a standard, the performance standards can be created through extended dialogue among teachers and teacher educators, grounded in concrete, complex, and contextualized examples of teaching practice. (p. 158)

THE BTSA ASSESSMENT SYSTEM

When California created the Beginning Teacher Support and Assessment (BTSA) system described in Chapter 6, assessment was a key component of the statewide program. There are two guiding documents for the BTSA program. The first is the *California Standards for the Teaching Profession* (CCTC and CDE, 1997) and the second is the *Standards of Quality and Effectiveness for Teacher Induction Programs* (California Commission on Teacher Credentialing, 2002). Standards for the teaching profession were discussed in Chapter 6. All induction activities are guided by these standards. The *Standards of Quality and Effectiveness for Teacher Induction Programs* are those guiding program sponsors that intend to offer an approved induction program that leads to a professional-level credential for teachers. Program sponsors prepare a program proposal that they submit to California Commission on Teacher Credentialing in order to be approved as an induction provider.

The schools or consortia that sponsor induction programs are required to include an assessment component that meets the requirements specified in *Standard 13: Formative Assessment Systems for Participating Teachers* (see Exhibit 7.1).

Exhibit 7.1 Program Standard 13: Formative Assessment Systems for
Participating Teachers

Each induction program's formative assessment system guides and informs
participating teachers about their own professional growth. The purpose of formative
assessment is to improve teaching, as measured by each standard of *The California
Standards for the Teaching Profession (CSTP)* and in relation to the state-adopted
academic content standards and performance levels for students. The results are
used to guide professional development. The formative assessment system is
characterized by multiple measures of teaching, collaboration with colleagues, focus
on classroom practice, and reflection together with a trained support provider about
evidence, using specific criteria. Participating teachers direct the uses of formative
assessment evidence generated from their teaching practice.

**Program Elements for Standard 13: Formative Assessment Systems for
Participating Teachers**

13(a) The program uses a formative assessment system that offers multiple
opportunities for participating teachers to learn and demonstrate knowledge,
understanding, and applications of *The California Standards for the Teaching
Profession* and the State adopted academic content standards and performance
levels for students in the context of their teaching assignments.

13(b) The formative assessment system provides for assessment monthly during the
school year of each participating teacher's classroom-based practice in relation
to the *CSTP* and to the state-adopted academic content standards and
performance levels for students. Assessment evidence is shared with each
participating teacher in a timely manner.

13(c) The assessment system includes multiple measures appropriate to the
standards being assessed to generate formative assessment evidence that is
consistent and accurate in relation to the *CSTP*. Multiple measures include
observation, the process of inquiry, and analyzing student work products.

13(d) Within the assessment system, criteria identify multiple levels of teaching
performance based on each element of the *CSTP* to formatively assess each
participating teacher's growth and practice.

13(e) The program includes a process for developing and implementing an
Individualized Induction Plan (IIP) for each participant, based on formative
assessment evidence, to document the support, extended preparation, and
professional growth of participating teachers. The IIP process begins with a
review of results from the teaching performance assessment, when available,
and then is used to document professional growth activities. The IIP is
informed by formative assessment information and completed during each
induction year.

13(f) The formative assessment system is characterized by:
   (i) Valid assessment instruments, including focused observations of and
        structured inquiries into teaching practice, designed to measure one or
        more elements of the *CSTP;*

(Continued)

Exhibit 7.1 (Continued)

(ii) *CSTP* element-specific criteria used to make professional judgments about teaching evidence;

(iii) Assessment evidence that includes both teacher work and student work and informs future practice in relation to the *CSTP* and to the state-adopted academic content standards and performance levels for students; and Standards of Quality and Effectiveness for Professional Teacher Induction Programs

(iv) A reflective process based on the *CSTP* that includes collaboration with support providers and other educators, as well as structured self-assessment, and informs future practice.

13(g) As directed by each participating teacher, formative assessment evidence may be presented as evidence for professional credential completion. Formative assessment results are used to guide professional development and not for the purpose of teacher evaluation or employment decisions.

13(h) The program implements a formal evaluation process to assess the effectiveness of the formative assessment system and to make improvements to the system and accompanying training.

Source: California Commission on Teacher Credentialing (2002), pp. 29–30

The development of the assessment component in BTSA has a long history. The pilot project that was a forerunner of BTSA, the California New Teacher Project, had included opportunities to pilot test not only the support strategies to be used, but also the newer performance-based assessment measures. Several prototypes were developed and evaluated for their costs, ease of use, and for the quality of information they provided. In the early years of BTSA, local programs were encouraged to subcontract with any appropriate assessment entity or to develop their own assessments. Assessments varied, as did the use of assessment information. In the most well-developed early programs, the results of assessment information was used by beginning teachers and their mentors to develop Individualized Induction Plans (IIPs) so that the support was appropriately targeted to assessed needs.

However, the structure for merging assessment data and support plans was not well developed in the early program plans. Individual program sponsors were not equally adept at making this happen for all teachers in their program. Some thought that to be assessed was somewhat threatening to new teachers and that it might even jeopardize the supportive relationship between new teacher and their support provider. Olebe (2001b) indicates that "support and assessment were treated as distinct, parallel, yet related aspects of new teacher induction" (p. 13).

To better merge support and assessment, the state agencies initiated a plan to develop a comprehensive system of this merged approach. With funding and personnel from Educational Testing Service, a design team of assessment experts and local program directors was formed. The resulting product, which consists of formative assessment events that combine observation and inquiry, is the California Formative Assessment and Support System for Teachers (CFASST). At the present time, the vast majority of programs use this system. Those programs that use an alternative system are required to demonstrate that they meet all of the elements described in Standard 13 (see Exhibit 7.1).

CFASST is a series of events designed to engage first- and second-year teachers in a series of tasks that include inquiries, classroom observations and individual professional development planning based on the *California Standards for the Teaching Profession*. Beginning teachers are also expected to apply California's Student Content Standards and Frameworks. With the guidance of their support provider (mentor), beginning teachers gather information about best practices, plan lessons, and receive feedback on their teaching. They reflect on their lessons, think about how to apply what they have learned to future lessons, and assess their teaching. A series of structured activities, called "events," leads the teacher through these investigations (Storms, Wing, Jinks, Banks, & Cavazos, 2000).

I reflect all the time, but it's internally. CFASST made me actually write it down and look at it. Reflecting on my growth—on the continuum really helps me.

First-year teacher
(McCormick, 2001, p. 60)

The CFASST system leads teachers though a series of assessment events that calls upon teachers to "plan, teach, reflect, and apply." Teachers are assessed on a four-point scale called Descriptions of Practice. Evidence is collected over time and examined against these Descriptions of Practice. Exhibit 7.2 outlines the elements in this system.

The system includes a comprehensive training program for those who will support beginning teachers and for those conducting formative assessment to improve practice. Those who are trained often indicate that the experience is powerful professional development for them as well, getting them to think about teaching in different ways. CFASST training includes

- Understanding the role of the support provider.
- Using the California Standards for the Teaching Profession to examine teaching.
- Investigating teaching through a structured inquiry process.
- Conducting classroom observations and providing feedback.

Exhibit 7.2 California Formative Assessment & Support System for Teachers

YEAR 1

1	2	3
CLASS, SCHOOL, DISTRICT AND COMMUNITY PROFILE (CSDC) Examine your context for teaching Select a subject-matter focus Select 2 students to follow	**INQUIRY: Establish an Environment for Student Learning** Examine feedback from an observation of your teaching Select a focus Develop and implement a plan Gather information Reflect on evidence Closure conference Consider IIP goals	**OBSERVATION: Profile of Practice I** Develop an instruction plan Examine feedback from an observation of your teaching Reflect on student learning Closure conference Develop IIP 1

4	5	6
INQUIRY: Assessing Instructional Experience Reflect on assessment Gather information Adapt an assessment strategy Teach and collect student work Reflect on student learning Closure conference Develop IIP 2	**OBSERVATION: Profile of Practice II** Develop an instruction plan Examine feedback from an observation of your teaching Reflect on student learning Closure conference Review progress on IIP goals	**SUMMARY OF PROFESSIONAL GROWTH** Review CFASST 1–5 Reflect on growth Identify insights and goals for next year Share in the colloquium of professional educators

YEAR 2

7	8	9
CLASS, SCHOOL, DISTRICT AND COMMUNITY PROFILE (CSDC) Examine your context for teaching Review student assessment data	**APPLYING FRAMEWORK TO PRACTICE** Review of the standards and framework Develop curriculum map Select student content standards Select 2 students to follow	**INQUIRY: Designing a Lesson Series** Examine student data Plan a week-long lesson series Teach the lessons Two observations Examine student data Closure conference

10	11	12
COMPONENTS OF EFFECTIVE INSTRUCTION	**INQUIRY: Assessing Student Learning Over Time**	**SUMMARY OF PROFESSIONAL GROWTH**
Complete self-assessment on components of effective instruction	Select student standards	Review CFASST I–II
Discuss evidence	Examine student data	Reflect on growth
Develop IIP 3	Select assessments	Identify insights and goals for next year
	Teach	Share in the colloquium of professional educators
	Assess student progress over time	
	Closure conference	

Source: Copyright 2001 by the California Commission on Teacher Credentialing and the California Department of Education. Portions copyrighted by Educational Testing Service. (CCTC and CDE, 2001)

- Comparing evidence to the Descriptions of Practice.
- Assessing teaching in relation to student achievement. (CCTC & CDE, 2001)

This training, while time-consuming and intensive, is essential to implementation of this complex, rich, assessment system. When assessors are well prepared for their work, the experience becomes richer for new and experienced teachers alike.

> I really like this program. . . . I find it to be positive and powerful. The support provider and beginning teacher grow reflective with the assessment piece.
>
> Induction program director
> (Tushnet et al., 2002, p. 15)

LOCALLY DEVELOPED ASSESSMENTS

Not every induction program will be in a state that has an assessment system in place to guide the induction period. Or perhaps, as is the case in California, the induction system allows for locally developed options. For those contemplating using an assessment teacher performance where states have no such requirement, these examples can be a guide to developing local assessments. The California Program Standards, particularly

Standard 13 (see Exhibit 7.1) outline the key elements of a standards-based formative assessment system.

In California, local assessment systems must meet the criteria listed in Standard 13. These criteria are useful for those in other states and localities who wish to design and implement formative assessments as a part of their induction programs.

USING ASSESSMENT TO ADVANCE REFLECTIVE PRACTICE

The CFASST and the INTASC assessments are designed to foster reflective practice in the early years of teaching and beyond. These two examples were presented as models that recognize the complexity of teaching and gather information that can be useful for reflective practice. They are authentic measures of teaching that takes place in a particular context.

Reflective practice is guided by such authentic assessments during the induction years. The INTASC standards and accompanying assessments stress the need for beginners to draw upon "professional literature, colleagues, and other resources to support his/her own development" and to use these resources for "reflection, problem solving and new ideas, actively sharing experiences and seeking and giving feedback" (INTASC, 1992, p. 32). In addition, INTASC calls for teachers to constantly assess the effects of their decisions and actions on students, parents, and other teachers, and to participate in "collegial activities designed to make the entire school a productive learning environment" (p. 36).

The California experience with induction has been grounded in a reflective stance, and assessment of teacher performance has long been considered an important tool to be used to help teachers reflect. However, early assessment efforts were not well integrated with the support system and the connections were not always made. With the development of a more standardized system of assessment, and rigorous training of support providers to use the assessment to inform support strategies, the program has brought the assessment component more fully into alignment with the support strategies being used with new teachers. Experienced teachers and new teachers work together to analyze, interpret, and reflect on the assessments to improve practice.

Performance-based assessments that are grounded in a rich conception of reflective teaching, such as the examples discussed here, show promise of improving the quality of teaching and learning in schools. Others who wish to develop assessment-driven induction systems can replicate the examples of INTASC and the CFASST assessments.

Such assessments are not without controversy. Porter et al. (2002) outline some of the tensions surrounding these new rich assessments:

- Tension exists between using assessments for accountability versus using them for teacher support and improvement.
- Tension exists between assessments that try to move the field forward, pressing for better teachers and better teacher education, versus those that are consistent with current practice, and that are, perhaps, more legally defensible.
- When assessment is used to make licensure decisions, tension exists between the goal of excellence and the fact that minimum competency is what is being established. (p. 294)

Many teachers could add their own lists of tensions around assessments in the induction years. Teachers want feedback about their work, but they want the feedback to be empowering, not stifling. They do not want assessments that add to their heavy workload, but that flow from and are integrated with work they are already doing. They want assessments that are useful to them, not intrusive. And finally, they want assessments that give them information about their work with their particular group of students.

It is worth the effort to work toward a resolution of these tensions to make assessments of teaching performance a vital part of the induction process. Assessments of teaching help to inform and guide practice, enrich the discussions of that practice, help shape and guide teaching of all teachers toward that vision of excellence.

IMPLICATIONS FOR PRACTICE

The main points of this chapter and their implications for practice can be summarized as follows:

1. Well-designed, standards-driven assessments of teaching performance help to inform new teachers and their mentors about how the new teachers are doing.

2. Assessments during the induction years can serve three purposes:
   - To control the movement of teachers into and out of positions at different stages of their careers.
   - To influence the performance and professional growth of teachers in particular positions.
   - To represent professional consensus about the knowledge and skills that teachers must have to engage in responsible practice.

3. Performance-based assessments are designed to measure teaching performance in authentic ways by using artifacts and examples of what teachers do in the classroom and evidence of how they think

about, plan for, and evaluate their work and the work of their students.

4. Beginning teachers and their mentors need to make the distinction between assessment and evaluation. Assessments refer to procedures, instruments, and protocols used to collect information about teacher performance. Evaluation refers to the purposes for which data and information are gathered.

5. The assessments of beginning teachers during an induction period should be considered in light of the range of assessments that are conducted of teachers during various points in their careers.

6. Induction programs use assessments for formative (to guide practice) and summative (to evaluate or make decisions) purposes.

7. While states vary in what assessments they use and the purposes for which they are used, there is a trend toward more assessment of teacher performance during the induction period.

8. Types of assessments of teaching include
   • Closed-ended or multiple-choice items
   • Student achievement gains
   • Student surveys about teaching effectiveness
   • Teacher surveys of practice
   • Portfolios
   • Teacher self-reports
   • Teachers interviews
   • Classroom observations
   • Open-ended items
   • Directed activities
   • Simulations exercises

9. Standard-based assessments have been development to accompany the INTASC standards and the California Standards for the Teaching Profession. These systems serve as examples for others who want to link standards and assessment in authentic ways.

10. Tensions around teacher assessment include
    • Accountability vs. support and improvement
    • Moving the profession forward vs. maintaining the status quo
    • Assessment for minimum competency vs. assessment to promote excellence
    • Assessments that requirement more work for teachers vs. embedded assessments
    • Assessments that are useful vs. assessments that are intrusive

11. Assessments of teaching help to inform and guide practice, enrich the discussions of that practice, help shape and guide teaching of all teachers toward that vision of excellence.

FOR FURTHER READING

Campbell, D. M., Melenyzer, B. J., Nettles, D. H., & Wyman, R. M. (2000). *Portfolio and performance assessment in teacher education.* Boston: Allyn and Bacon.
This is a book for those who want to develop a performance-based assessment system using the portfolio approach. It covers the following:
1. Establishing and communication program parameters
2. Maintaining quality in both learning and documentation of learning
3. Supporting and enabling students in their professional and portfolio development
4. Developing a cohesive and comprehensive plan for program evaluation and continuous improvement

Carr, J. F. & Harris, D. E. (2001). *Succeeding with standards: Linking curriculum, assessment, and action planning.* Alexandria, VA: Association for Supervision and Curriculum Development.
This book covers the key components of standards linking. It includes understanding the vision, assessing the current state of affairs, developing a curriculum and assessment plan, making some important school curriculum, decisions related to the standards, garnering resources, developing a professional development plan, providing appropriate supervision and evaluation, collecting student assessment information, developing a comprehensive assessment system, providing regular reports of progress, and developing and implementing an action plan.

Glatthorn, A. A. (1999). *Performance standards and authentic learning.* Larchmont, NY: Eye on Education.
This practical guide for classroom teachers demonstrates how to implement a standards-based curriculum, develop performance tasks, teach to those tasks, and provide students with authentic learning. It focuses on foundational knowledge, planning for excellence, and teaching for success.

Solomon, P. G. (2002). *Assessment bridge: Positive ways to link tests to learning, standards, and curriculum improvement.* Thousand Oaks, CA: Corwin.
Today's high-stakes standards-based testing movement seems to compromise effective teaching and learning rather than improve it. Committed teachers know the importance of student assessment as a guide to classroom instruction. Restoring assessment to its proper place in the curriculum is the goal of this clear-headed analysis. Chapters cover
- The origins and history of the current testing movement
- How good tests guide teaching and learning
- How to balance standardized tests, curriculum standards, and critical local variables such as class size, socioeconomics, and teacher attitudes
- How to build bridges from test anxiety to improved student learning, teacher training, curriculum and instruction, and school administration and leadership
- How to recruit, train, and nurture a new generation of talented, committed, and effective teachers

8

Developing Induction Policies to Shape Induction Practices

Teacher induction is beginning to be recognized as a special period in the development of the teacher. Induction programs help to retain teachers and lead to their success. However, induction programs need to be institutionalized in state and local policies as a permanent part of the learning to teach continuum. National and state policies regarding induction practices will be most successful if they allowing for tailoring of induction practices to fit local needs and contexts. This chapter focuses on what we have learned about induction policies and practices and where induction may be headed in the future.

A VISION OF TEACHER INDUCTION

This book has focused on induction as a developmental process for new teachers, one that is grounded in a view of the teacher as a reflective practitioner. Teaching expertise develops over time as teachers engage in, examine, refine, and develop and grow into expert teaching.

Teacher needs in the early years are quite complex and highly varied. Because the background and prior learning of new teachers differs so greatly, their needs differ as well. In Chapter 1, a summary of the typical procedural, managerial, psychological, instructional, professional, cultural, and political needs of teachers addressed in induction program planning was presented.

Within these broad areas, there are differences among individual teachers in terms of what are their most pressing needs and where they need the most assistance. Induction program planners need to be attuned to the range of concerns in each area outlined above. They also need to be concerned about the needs unarticulated or not expressed.

The first three categories of needs—those of procedures, management tasks, and psychological issues—tend to consume the focus of the teacher who is still at the survival level. This is the teacher who functions on a day-to-day basis, is primarily guided by the text and the teacher's guide, and is still working out systems of classroom management.

As teachers advance along the continuum of development, their needs shift to the instructional, professional, cultural, and political arenas. They become more focused on improving and refining instructional practices, diagnosing and meeting individual student's needs, gaining awareness of their students and their families, and finding their place in the profession of teaching. Although certain aspects of each of these areas need to be addressed right from the start (such as making sure that teachers understand curriculum standards and expectations), these areas are difficult to address in a nuanced and sophisticated way with the teacher who still struggles with survival level need.

Sometimes novice teachers have difficulty identifying and articulating their own needs and the needs of their students. Or they may misidentify the problem because they do not fully understand their own shortcomings. Worse yet, they blame the students themselves for their failure to learn. Because the learning gaps are most pronounced in our large, urban schools, our most needy students are most impacted when teachers are not fully committed to improving their instructional performance. All students need to have the opportunity to learn through a culturally relevant, demanding curriculum.

The role of the mentor is to help these novices see their own teaching more clearly, identify the practices that are successful, and help them remove the barriers to learning for their students. As teachers reflect on practice and the impact they are having on students, they learn to carefully and critically examine what they are doing, why they are doing it, and what students are learning or not learning. The mentor is a guide in those reflections, helping teachers see beyond their limited perspectives to focus on improved student performance.

Standards for the teaching profession and standards for students ground those discussions in some agreed-upon definitions of what is that teachers should know and be able to do and what students ought to be learning. We realize that not all teachers will meet the standards in the same way or reach the same level of expertise. Teachers realize that it is important that they are making progress towards attainment of those teaching standards and that students make progress toward achieving standards for set out for them.

Assessments of teaching practice can help more clearly define and clarify those needs and provide authentic evidence of practice. They help us understand what teachers actually do in the course of their work. Teachers and their mentors look at the evidence together and plan for the new teacher's future professional development.

The teacher develops an induction plan in consultation with the mentor. The induction plan is the first step in planning for the teachers professional development needs. This kind of induction experience leads quite naturally to the continued growth and learning of the teacher throughout her professional life.

TEACHER AND STUDENT SUCCESS

Induction has been traditionally conceived as a way to improve teacher retention. For many, this is still the primary focus. Retention is important, because high turnover rates have a devastating impact on schools and on students. High turnover is costly to the state and to the district as well, because it is expensive to educate, recruit, and initiate a new teacher. According to one estimate, it costs taxpayers more than $50,000 when a teacher leaves the profession (Texas State Board for Educator Certification, 1998). Money spent on inducting that same teacher, even at the rich resource level of the California model, is a very cost-effective investment of resources. In fact, California discovered that the investment in induction was recovered in a few short years with increased retention (California Commission on Teacher Credentialing & California Department of Education, 1992).

However, improved retention of teachers is only one reason for continuing to give attention to a well-designed and delivered induction experience for new teachers. Perhaps more importantly, we know that such programs can actually improve the teacher's ability to teach and help them become more proficient at an earlier point in their careers.

Good teaching results in improved student learning. If induction activities challenge teachers to critically examine their own practice and reflect on what they students are learning, we can help students by helping their teachers. However, to have that impact, induction needs to focus specifically on practices that enhance learning. Induction programs need to include but move beyond self-initiated issues and concerns about survival that too often characterized early induction efforts. It needs to be standards driven and move beyond the emotional support that once dominated induction activities. It needs to move beyond the fear of contaminating the nurturing support role of mentors by introducing thoughtful assessments of practice.

LOCAL INDUCTION POLICIES

A district or even a local school can develop its own plan for the induction of new teachers. Policies related to induction need to be clearly defined. Whether the district is a part of a state induction or is developing its own induction plan, the local context shapes induction needs and planning.

Districts or schools will want to develop plans that reflect their needs, preference, and priorities. Exhibit 8.1 lists questions that need to be addressed in developing policies for local plans.

STATE POLICY

At one time, teacher education policies at the state level were narrowly focused on entry-level criteria, or the initial license to practice. Most states now have policies that address teacher development as a continuum that spans the teacher's career from preservice through their ongoing professional development. These policies recognize the complexity of teaching and the need to ensure that teachers are not only minimally qualified at entry, but continue that development throughout their career.

State policies have only recently recognized the importance of the induction years as a unique phase of teacher development. Policies vary from state-to-state, as do funding levels for these programs. Some policies focus primarily on the assessments that take place during the induction period, while others focus on the development of an infrastructure for support and mentoring. Some states, such as California, attempt to do both.

Within most state policy frameworks, alternate routes into this system are sanctioned and controlled by minimum expectations for entry and timelines for completion. These policies also vary widely from one state to another.

While the definitions of "alternate routes" vary, the component most often left out of the alternative programs is the intensive, sustained period of student or practice teaching under the guidance of an experienced teacher.

It is now quite rare for a teacher to be issued a license that will be valid throughout their career without further study or professional development. Most states require that teachers complete credential renewal requirements as a way to encourage continued learning and development.

Because induction is still emerging as a new part of this state policy structure, the eventual shape of the policies guiding this new period remains unclear. Many questions remain about the state role in this crucial period of development. One primary issue yet to be resolved is the balance between state direction and local control over the delivery of induction services. Another concern is the balance between induction for teacher support and induction for teacher accountability.

What is lacking in many states' plans for induction is the recognition that teachers who are being inducted into the profession enter through an

Exhibit 8.1 Questions Addressed in Local Induction Program Planning

Initial planning	How many new teachers will be needed? In what areas? How many mentors will be needed? Who will lead the program? Who will be involved in the program? What will be their roles and responsibilities? How will educational partners, such as the local universities, be involved? How will participants be prepared for their roles? What resources will be available to support the program? What will be considered the induction period? What are the overall goals of this program?
Recruiting	How will teachers be recruited, interviewed, and hired to find the most qualified teachers who are a good match? How can the induction program be used as an incentive to recruit new teachers?
Assignments	How will teachers be assigned to classrooms? How will their workloads reflect their novice status?
Orienting	What kind and length of orientation will new teachers receive? Who will be involved? How will the content or the orientation be structured to best introduce teachers to their new responsibilities?
Mentoring	Who will be the mentors? How will they be selected? How will they be trained? How will they be matched with new teachers? How many new teachers will they serve? What are the expectations for their mentoring roles? How and when will they work with new teachers? How will they be compensated for their work? How will they be supported in their work? What kind ongoing professional development will they receive? How will their work with new teachers be evaluated? How will they work with site administrators to support new teachers?
Professional development	What professional development activities will be a part of the induction program? What will be required and what will be optional? How can professional development be tailored to individual needs? How can professional development be tailored to the local context? How can teachers meet with other teachers who share their grade level/content area interests? How can professional development associated with other reform efforts be integrated with the induction plan? How will the professional development offerings be evaluated?
Assessing new teacher progress	How will new teacher progress be assessed? How will assessments of progress be shared and discussed with the new teacher? How will assessments contribute to reflective practice? How will these assessments help to shape and improve teaching practice and student learning?
Evaluating the induction program	How will each aspect of the induction program be evaluated to determine if program goals are being met? What impacts will the program have on new teachers? On their students? On experienced teachers who serve as mentors?

ever-increasing variety of routes and pathways. Induction policies cannot mandate one plan or set of policies for everyone. Not every new teacher is brand new to the workforce. A career changer has different needs than does a young new teacher just out of college. Not every new teacher begins teaching after completing a full program of studies in preparation to teach. The academically prepared teacher has different needs than the alternate-route teacher. Not every new teacher in a particular school or district is new to the profession. A teacher who has taught in one state and moves to another to teach has different needs than the teacher who has already taught in a different context. A teacher who has taught middle school and moves to high school has different needs than a teacher who is beginning high school teaching. A teacher who has taught in an isolated rural area and begins a new position in an urban environment will have different needs than the brand new urban teacher with no other experience.

It remains for those implementing induction at the local levels to sort out the differences among all of their "beginners" and to offer a flexible range of opportunities that will help all of their teachers succeed.

This argues for a customized approach to teacher induction, one that recognized multiple pathways into the profession and a variety of needs that individuals might bring. It also argues for some discretion at the local level to determine how best to meet the needs of their own teachers in their own contexts.

THE CONTINUUM OF DEVELOPMENT IN CALIFORNIA

California, because of its size, complexity, and diversity is often a bellwether state in policies relating to education. In the last two decades, we have learned, and are continuing to learn, much about this newly recognized formal phase of teacher development in California. The state has invested heavily in funding induction and in evaluating its effects.

California's policy makers have also given careful thought to the full developmental continuum of learning to teach. Exhibit 8.2 illustrates the model that has emerged. California's Learning to Teach System has been designed to provide alternative routes to earning a teaching credential that meet the needs of candidates at various levels. California recognizes that there are multiple pathways or routes to entry into the profession, but that each route ought to be guided by the same standards. All routes are guided by the same standards (California Standards for the Teaching Profession), or expectations, that teachers will meet. These standards, and the related student standards, shape the professional development for teachers and the mentoring conversations that take place among novices and their more experienced colleagues. The standards connect the parts of the system.

Exhibit 8.2

California's Learning to Teach System

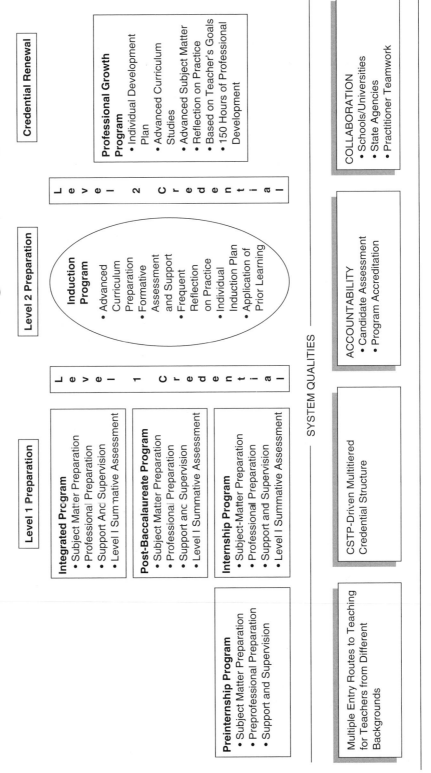

Level 1 Preparation

Integrated Program
- Subject Matter Preparation
- Professional Preparation
- Support And Supervision
- Level I Summative Assessment

Post-Baccalaureate Program
- Subject Matter Preparation
- Professional Preparation
- Support and Supervision
- Level I Summative Assessment

Internship Program
- Subject-Matter Preparation
- Professional Preparation
- Support and Supervision
- Level I Summative Assessment

Preinternship Program
- Subject Matter Preparation
- Preprofessional Preparation
- Support and Supervision

Level 1 Credential

Level 2 Preparation

Induction Program
- Advanced Curriculum Preparation
- Formative Assessment and Support
- Frequent Reflection on Practice
- Individual Induction Plan
- Application of Prior Learning

Level 2 Credential

Credential Renewal

Professional Growth Program
- Individual Development Plan
- Advanced Curriculum Studies
- Advanced Subject Matter
- Reflection on Practice
- Based on Teacher's Goals
- 150 Hours of Professional Development

SYSTEM QUALITIES

Multiple Entry Routes to Teaching for Teachers from Different Backgrounds

CSTP-Driven Multitiered Credential Structure

ACCOUNTABILITY
- Candidate Assessment
- Program Accreditation

COLLABORATION
- Schools/Universities
- State Agencies
- Practitioner Teamwork

There are varying levels of programs—staged for appropriate level of development and stage of career. Accountability and appropriate assessments are built into each level. The entire system requires extensive collaboration among schools and universities so that teacher development is addressed in a consistent and coherent manner throughout the continuum of development.

California is not the only state to move in this direction. Other states are incorporating this induction period into their licensing systems in other ways. Most are driven by a well-defined set of standards or expectations for teachers and linked to student standards in this era of accountability. Most are looking at induction as a period that can help address the growing teacher shortage as well as focus efforts on improving teacher quality.

We know that a planned induction period of the intensity described in this book can lead to better retention of teachers and improved teaching practices. However, because induction is a relatively new concept and induction funding is not always secure, uncertainly about its permanent place in the learning to teach continuum remains. Implementation efforts have been sporadic and very much dependent upon the commitment of individuals charged with delivery of services at the school level. Even with the extensive funding available in California, there are still teachers who are not being served or who are not served very well.

Most states realize that induction is relevant to all schools, but that it has special relevance in urban settings that experience higher-than-average rates of turnover and that hire larger numbers of underprepared teachers than do their neighboring districts. Special attention needs to be paid to these districts in the development of state policies.

Questions of resources remain. The amount of money available for induction programs varies widely. Some states mandate induction but do not fund it. Others fund it at a very insignificant level. California, to this point, has had rich funding for its induction programs, providing $3300 per teacher (with a $2000 district match) in the 2003–2004 fiscal year. However, the future of support for induction remains uncertain as the state faces declining revenues. Resources are required if the program is to delivery the kinds of high-intensity services that make a difference for new teachers.

THE FEDERAL ROLE

Although the states have legal authority and responsibility for providing education to children and youth, and for developing the policies that guide educational matters, the federal government uses its power to influence and, through funding mechanisms, its resources, to shape educational policy in states and localities. Recently, the federal government has weighed in on matters of teacher quality. As a part of the *No Child Left Behind Act,* Congress issued the challenge to states and local districts to ensure that by the end of the 2005–2006 school year every classroom in America has a teacher who is "highly qualified." Although general guidelines for determining who indeed meets the definition of highly qualified, states are charged with submitting a plan that fits their own state systems (U.S. Department of Education, 2002).

The federal government has chosen to focus its attention on knowledge of subject matter rather than pedagogy or practice. It encourages alternate certification plans for individuals who can demonstrate on a test that they know and understand the subject matter. Consequently, those alternate-route teachers, who are still acquiring knowledge of teaching and learning about pedagogy while they teach, are deemed to be, by the federal definition, "highly qualified." Yet some of these alternative-route teachers are also underprepared in many ways. The federal government recognizes that these teachers need to be enrolled in a formal, alternative-preparation program. The paradox of the highly qualified, underprepared teacher illustrates the complexities of encouraging alternative routes into teaching while maintaining high professional expectations and standards.

Another nationalizing force in teacher quality issues is the voluntary national accreditation system under the auspices of the National Council on Accreditation for Teacher Education (NCATE). In its accreditation policies, NCATE has been moving toward a model of holding institutions of higher education accountable for measuring the results and the impacts of their programs on their candidates and the students that are served by these teachers.

Although induction, per se, is not a focus of accreditation, institutions are obliged to follow up on their candidates in the field, into the induction period. The linkages with graduates and the need to follow their progress in the early years have also focused university attention on teacher induction practices, if they were not already involved in local induction partnerships.

The Interstate New Teacher Assessment and Support Consortium (INTASC) standards for beginning teachers, discussed in Chapter 6, have become a recognized part of the NCATE standards, helping to spread their dissemination and increase the recognition that standards-based practice is important to maintaining teacher quality. Professional standards that cut across state lines and across credentialing systems help to establish a wider recognition of the fact that teachers are being inducted into a profession that holds its members accountable for their practice.

FROM POLICY TO PRACTICE

It is one thing to develop the policies, standards, and guidelines for teacher induction, yet quite another to put them into practice in ways that meet the professional development needs of all teachers. Induction takes place in a local context, school-by-school and teacher-by-teacher. It is highly dependent on what a given teacher needs at a particular point in time in the context of a particular classroom.

However much we have learned about this newly recognized formal phase of teacher development, there is more to be learned. In districts and schools that implement induction programs, the same programs can be successful with one teacher but not another. We know that intensive mentoring makes a difference, but we know less about what aspects of mentoring are most helpful. We know deep, rich, reflective conversations about teaching are important, but we know less about how those reflective conversations help to expand knowledge and shape teaching practice. While we know that better, more sophisticated teaching practice leads to improved student learning, we know less about how this happens or what induction experiences have the most impact on student learning.

Even when we know what needs to be done, we continue to face implementation challenges. One challenge is the match of appropriate mentors and new teachers. The best mentors may not be located at the same site as the new teachers or may not be a match by grade level or disciplinary area. Some mentoring pairs work better than others. How can we ensure that we have made the best possible matches?

Induction research and practice has been generically focused on teaching in general. We know and understand good induction and mentoring practices. Do they differ by discipline or by grade level? Is induction of the fourth-grade teacher different in some way than induction of the tenth-grade science teacher? Are there different induction needs and approaches to use with special education teachers? The work on induction for specific disciplines and specific specialty areas is just beginning.

Another challenge is that of the competing programs and practices within schools that demand time and energy from those who are asked to focus on induction. Induction tends to get lost in the maze of other priorities. It may be one program or one reform among many. How do we make induction a priority? How do we integrate induction with other new initiatives and other professional development activities? How do these efforts interact? How do we ensure that enough time and energy are spent on new teachers?

Some, but certainly not the majority of induction programs have begun to use technology as an important tool in induction programs. Technology can be used as a way to connect teachers with each other and with a vast source of professional resources. Program information posted on a web site can keep everyone well informed.

All teachers need to be inducted into a context that supports their work and leads to student success. We know that the school culture is important to a good induction experience. Some schools are characterized by culture that is collegial and innovative. These are places where teachers work together to solve problems and explore new ideas. They keep the focus on student learning and work to mobilize people and other resources to ensure that a high level of learning takes place. Other schools are marked by poor morale, teachers who practice independent of one another, and students who continue to fall further behind. How do we change the culture of schools to make them more receptive to new teachers and environments that support the learning and growth of not only new teachers, but all teachers?

The large number of underprepared teachers who enter teaching, require a different delivery system for induction activities than the more traditionally prepared teacher. How do we effectively stage preparation and induction when they occur concurrently rather than sequentially? How do we integrate the learning experiences so that they are mutually supportive rather than disjointed and disconnected?

These are some of the challenges to induction that need to be addressed more fully.

THE FUTURE OF INDUCTION

Teacher induction appears to be more than the "latest trend" in education. It's growing attention in schools, universities, and state legislatures has been noticeable. Careful attention to teachers' induction experiences today can help to retain and shape the workforce of the future.

Induction can bring together all who have in interest in teacher quality. Legislators at the state and national level are concerned about teacher retention and teacher quality. Universities want to see that their candidates are successful once they enter the field. Districts and local schools want to retain those whom they hire and want them to be successful. Teachers want colleagues who work collaboratively to improve teaching and learning in their schools. Parents want high-quality, thoughtful teachers for their children.

Too many induction programs have been inadequately funded and short-lived. If induction is to achieve its full potential, it needs to be fully supported. Policies need to be put into place in all states to make induction a permanent part of the learning-to-teach continuum. Induction needs a place in the system along with the notion of preparation and professional growth requirements. Induction needs focus on moving teachers—all teachers—beyond survival to success and high-quality teaching.

IMPLICATIONS FOR PRACTICE

The main points of this chapter and their implications for practice can be summarized as follows:

1. An understanding of the specific needs of new teachers will help induction planners to better meet those needs.

2. The role of the mentor is to help novices see their own teaching more clearly and to reflect on the impact their teaching has on learners.

3. Assessments of teaching practice can help to more clearly define and clarify those needs and provide authentic evidence of practice.

4. The primary goals of induction are retention and improved teacher performance.

5. Local policies related to induction need to be clearly defined.

6. Many states have policies related to teacher induction as a distinct phase of the learning-to-teach continuum.

7. Induction of alternate-route teachers is not often well addressed and should be considered in induction planning.

8. New teachers will have different learning needs based on their background, their position, and the context. State policies and practices related to induction do not always capture this complexity of induction needs.

9. California's learning-to-teaching continuum offers a model for state policies related to teacher preparation, induction, and professional development.

10. Adequate resources need to be available for induction programs.

11. Federal policies impact induction planning in important ways.

12. National accreditation policies impact induction efforts and help to standardize a vision of competent teaching.

13. Interest in induction is growing and can bring together diverse groups who all have an interest in teacher quality.

References

Achinstein, B., & Barrett, A. (2003, April). *(Re)framing classroom contexts: How new teachers and mentor view diverse learners and challenges of practice.* Paper presented at the Annual Conference of the American Educational Research Association, Chicago.

Ayers, W., & Ford, P. (Eds.). (1996). *City kids: City teachers.* New York: New Press.

Ball, D. L., & Cohen, D. K. (1999). Developing practice, developing practitioners: Toward a practice-based theory of professional education. In L. Darling-Hammond & G. Sykes (Eds.), *Teaching as the learning profession: Handbook of policy and practice.* San Francisco: Jossey-Bass.

Bartell, C. A. (2004, April), *Beginning to teach in the urban middle school.* Paper presented at the Annual Conference of the American Educational Research Association, San Diego.

Bartell, C. A. (1995). Shaping teacher induction policy in California. *Teacher Education Quarterly, 22*(4), 27–43.

Benson, B. P. (2003). *How to meet standards, motivate students, and still enjoy teaching: Four practices that improve student learning.* Thousand Oaks, CA: Corwin Press.

Berliner, D. C. (1994). The wonders of exemplary performance. In J. N. Mangieri & C. C. Block (Eds.), *Creating powerful thinking in teachers and students.* Fort Worth: Harcourt Brace.

Biddle, B. J., & Berliner, D. C. (2002). Small class size and its effects. *Educational Leadership, 59*(5), 12–23.

Brown, D. F. (2002). *Becoming a successful urban teacher.* Portsmouth, NH: Heinemann.

Burden, P. W. (1980). *Teachers' perceptions of the characteristics and influences on their personal and professional development.* Manhattan, KS: Author. (ERIC Document Reproduction Service No. ED198087)

Calderhead, J. (1992). The role of reflection in learning to teach. In L. Valli (Ed.), *Reflective teacher education: Causes and critiques.* Albany, NY: State University of New York Press.

California Commission on Teacher Credentialing (CCTC) & California Department of Education (CDE). (1992). *Success for beginning teachers.* Sacramento, CA: Author.

California Commission on Teacher Credentialing (CCTC) & California Department of Education (CDE). (1997). *California standards for the teaching profession.* Sacramento, CA: Author.http://www.ctc.ca.gov

California Commission on Teacher Credentialing (CCTC) & California Department of Education (CDE). (2001). *The CFASST process.* Sacramento, CA: Author.

California Commission on Teacher Credentialing (CCTC)(2002). *Standards of quality and effectiveness for teacher induction programs.* Sacramento, CA: Author.

Cibulka, J. G., Reed, R. J., & Wong, K. K. (1992). *The politics of urban education in the United States.* Washington, DC: Falmer.

Clark, C.M., & Peterson, P. L. (1986). Teachers' thought processes. In M. C. Whittrock (Ed.), *Handbook of research on teaching,* 3rd ed. New York: Macmillan.

Crosby, E. A. (1999). Urban schools forced to fail. *Phi Delta Kappan, 81*(4), 298–303.

Daresh, J. D. (2003). *Teachers mentoring teachers: A practical approach to helping new and experienced staff.* Thousand Oaks, CA: Corwin.

Darling-Hammond, L. (1997). *The right to learn.* San Francisco: Jossey-Bass.

Darling-Hammond, L. (1999). Teacher recruitment, selection, and induction: Policy influences on the supply and quality of teachers. In L. Darling-Hammond & G. Sykes (Eds.), *Teaching as the learning profession: Handbook of policy and practice.* San Francisco: Jossey-Bass.

Darling-Hammond, L. (2001). Standard setting in teaching: Changes in licensing, certification, and assessment. In V. Richardson (Ed.), *Handbook of research on teaching,* 4th ed. Washington, DC: American Educational Research Association.

Darling-Hammond, L. (2003). Keeping good teachers: Why it matters, what leaders can do. *Educational Leadership, 6*(8), 6–13.

Darling-Hammond, L., Wise, A. E., & Klein, S. P. (1999). *A license to teach: Raising standards for teaching.* San Francisco: Jossey-Bass.

Dewey, J. (1933). *How we think: A restatement of the relation of reflective thinking to the educative process.* New York: D.C. Heath and Co.

Dimock, G. E. (1989). *The unity of the Odyssey.* Amherst: The University of Massachusetts Press.

Doolittle, F., Herlihy, C., & Snipes, J. (2002). *Foundations for success: Case studies of how urban school systems improve student achievement.* New York: MDRC.

Elmore, R. F. (1983). Complexity and control: What legislators and administrators can do about implementing public policy. In L. S. Shulman & G. Sykes (Eds.), *Handbook of teaching and policy.* New York: Longman.

Erickson, E. H. (1963). *Childhood and society.* New York: Norton.

Erickson, E. H. (1982). *The life cycle completed.* New York: Norton.

Feiman-Nemser, S. (1983). Learning to teach. In L. S. Shulman & Gary Sykes (Eds.), *Handbook of research on teaching and policy.* New York: Longman.

Feiman-Nemser, S. (1990). Teacher preparation: Structural and conceptual alternatives. In W. R. Houston (Ed.), *Handbook of research on teacher education.* New York: Macmillan.

Feiman-Nemser, S. (1996). *Teacher mentoring: A critical review.* ERIC Document Reproduction Service No. ED397060.

Feiman-Nemser, S. (2001). Helping novices learn to teach: Lessons from an exemplary support teacher. *Journal of Teacher Education, 52*(1), 17–30.

Feiman-Nemser, S. (2003). What new teachers need to learn. *Educational Leadership, 60*(8), 25–29.

Feiman-Nemser, S., & Floden, R. E. (1986). The cultures of teaching. In M. C. Whittrock (Ed.), *Handbook of research on teaching,* 3rd ed. New York: Macmillan.

Feistritzer, C. E. (1993). National overview of alternative teacher certification. *Education and Urban Society, 26*(1), 18–28.

Fendler, L. (2003). Teacher reflection in a hall of mirrors: Historical influences and political reverberations. *Educational Researcher, 32*(3), 16–25.

Fessler, R., & Christiansen, J. (1992). *The teacher career cycle: Understanding and guiding the professional development of teachers.* Boston: Allyn & Bacon.

Fideler, E. F., & Haselkorn, D. (1999). *Learning the ropes: Urban teacher induction programs and practice in the United States.* Belmont, MA: Recruiting New Teachers.

Fisher, C. J., Fox, D. L., & Paille, E. (1996). Teacher education research in the English language arts and reading. In J. Sikula (Ed.), *Handbook of research on teacher education,* 2nd ed. New York: Simon & Schuster Macmillan.

Fuller, F. F. (1969). Concerns of teachers: A developmental conceptualization. *American Educational Research Journal, 6*(2), 207–225.

Gold, Y. (1996). Beginning teacher support: Attrition, mentoring, and induction. In J. Sikula (Ed.) *Handbook of research on teacher education,* 2nd ed. New York: Simon & Schuster Macmillan.

Goldberg, P. E., & Proctor, K. M. (2000). *Teacher voices: A survey on teacher recruitment and retention. Scholastic.* Retrieved from http://teacher.scholastic.com/professional/teachertoteacher/ttt/voices_part_1.pdf

Guyton, E., & Hidalgo, F. (1995). Characteristics, responsibilities, and qualities of urban school mentors. *Education and Urban Society, 28*(1), 40–47.

Haberman, M. (1994). Gentle teaching in a violent society. *Educational Horizons, 72*(3), 1–13.

Haberman, M. (1996). Selecting and preparing culturally competent teachers for urban schools. In J. Sikula (Ed.), *Handbook of research on teacher education,* 2nd ed. New York: Simon & Schuster Macmillan.

Harris and Associates, Inc. (1991). *The Metropolitan Life survey of the American teacher, 1991. The first year: New teachers' expectations and ideals.* New York: Author.

Hawley, W. D. & Valli, L. (1999). The essentials of effective professional development: A new consensus. In L. Darling-Hammond & G. Sykes (Eds.), *Teaching as the learning profession: Handbook of policy and practice.* San Francisco: Jossey-Bass.

Henke, R. R., Choy, S. P., Chen, X., Geis, S., Alt, M. N., & Broughman, S. P. (1997). *America's teachers: Profile of a profession, 1993–1994.* (U.S. Department of Education, National Center for Education Statistics NCES 97–460). Washington, DC: U.S. Government Printing Office.

Henry, M. (1989). Change in teacher education: Focus on field experiences. In J. Braun (Ed.), *Reforming teacher education: Issues and directions.* New York: Garland Press.

Houston, W. R., Marshall, F., & McDavid, T. (1993). Problems of traditionally prepared and alternatively certified first-year teachers. *Education and Urban Society, 26*(1), 78–89.

Huberman, M. (1989). The professional life cycle of teachers. *Teachers College Record, 91*(1), 31–58.

Huberman, M. (1993). Linking the practitioner and researcher communities for school improvement. *School Effectiveness and School Improvement, 4*(1), 1–16.

Huling-Austin, L. (1992). Research on learning to teach: Implications for teacher induction and mentoring programs. *Journal of Teacher Education, 43*(3), 173–180.

Huling-Austin, L., Odell, S. J., Ishler, P., Kay, R. S., & Edelfelt, R. A. (Eds.). (1989). *Assisting the beginning teacher*. Reston, VA: Association of Teacher Educators.

Ingersoll, R. M. (2001). Teacher turnover and teacher shortages: An organizational analysis. *American Educational Research Journal, 38*(3), 499–534.

Interstate New Teacher Assessment and Support Consortium (INTASC) (1992). *Model standards for beginning teacher licensing and development: A resource for state dialogue*. Washington, DC: Council of Chief State School Officers. http://www.ccsso.org

Interstate New Teacher Assessment and Support Consortium (INTASC). (1995a). *Mathematics teaching performance assessment handbook*. Washington, DC: Council of Chief State School Officers.

Interstate New Teacher Assessment and Support Consortium (INTASC). (1995b). *Next steps: Moving toward performance-based licensing in teaching*. Washington, DC: Council of Chief State School Officers.

Johnson, S. M. (1986). Incentives for teachers: What motivates, what matters? *Educational Administration Quarterly, 22*(3), 54–79.

Joyce, B. R., & Showers, B. (2002). *Student achievement through staff development*, 3rd ed. Alexandria, VA: Association for Supervision and Curriculum Development.

Katz, L. (1979). *Helping others learn to teach: Some principles and techniques for inservice educators*. Urbana, IL: ERIC Clearinghouse on Early Childhood Education.

Kemmis, S., & McTaggart, R. (1988). *The action research planner*, 3rd ed. Geelong, Australia: Deakin University Press.

Kent, K. M. (1993). The need for school-based teacher reflection. *Teacher Education Quarterly, 20*(1), 83–91.

Knowles, M. S., Holton, E. F., & Swanson, R. A. (1998). *The adult learner*, 5th ed. Houston: Butterworth Heinemann.

Kruse, S. D., Louis, K. S., & Bryk, A. S. (1995). An emerging framework for analyzing school-based professional community. In K. S. Louis & S. D. Kruse (Eds.), *Professionalism and community: Perspectives on reforming urban schools*. Thousand Oaks, CA: Corwin.

Lieberman, A. (1988). *Building a professional culture in schools*. New York: Teachers College Press.

Lindsey, R. B., Nuri Robins, K., Terrell, R. D. (2003). *Cultural proficiency: A manual for school leaders*. Thousand Oaks, CA: Corwin.

Little, J. W. (1987). Teachers as colleagues. In V. Richardson-Koehler (Ed.), *Educator's handbook: Research and practice*. New York: Longman.

Little, J. W. (1990). The persistence of privacy: Autonomy and initiative in teachers' professional relations. *Teachers College Record, 91*(4), 509–536.

Little, J. W. (1999). Organizing schools for teacher learning. In L. Darling-Hammond & G. Sykes (Eds.), *Teaching as the learning profession: Handbook of policy and practice*. San Francisco: Jossey-Bass.

Mager, G. M. (1992). The place of induction in becoming a teacher. In G. P. DeBolt (Ed.), *Teacher induction and mentoring: School-based collaborative programs*. Albany, NY: State University of New York Press.

McCormick, R. S. (2001). Is it just natural? Beginning teachers' growth in reflective practice. *Issues in Teacher Education, 10*(2), 55–67.

Metropolitan Life Insurance Company (2001). *Survey of the American teacher, 2001: Key elements of quality schools*. Author: New York.

Moir, E. (1999). The stages of a teacher's first year. In M. Scherer (Ed.), *A better beginning: Supporting and mentoring new teachers.* Alexandria, VA: Association for Supervision and Curriculum Development.

Moir E., Gless, J., & Baron, W. (1999). A support program with heart: The Santa Cruz project. In M. Scherer (Ed.), *A better beginning: Supporting and mentoring new teachers.* Alexandria, VA: Association for Supervision and Curriculum Development.

Moss, P.A., Schutz, A.M., & Collins, K. (1998). An interpretative approach to portfolio evaluation of teacher licensure. *Journal for Personnel Evaluation. 12*(2), 193–161.

National Association of State Directors of Teacher Education and Certification (NASDTEC). (2002). *The NASDTEC manual on the preparation and certification of educational personnel,* 7th ed. Sacramento, CA: School Services.

National Commission on Teaching and America's Future (NCTAF). (1996). *What matters most: Teaching for America's future.* New York: Author.

National Council on Accreditation of Teacher Education (NCATE). (2002). *Professional standards for the accreditation of schools, colleges, and departments of education.* Washington, DC: Author.

Odell, S. J., & Huling, L. (Eds.). (2000). *Quality mentoring for novice teachers.* Indianapolis, IN: Kappa Delta Pi.

Olebe, M. G. (2001a). A decade of policy support for California's new teachers: The beginning teacher support and assessment program. *Teacher Education Quarterly, 28*(1), 71–84.

Olebe, M. G. (2001b). Can policy mandate teacher reflection? *Issues in Teacher Education, 10*(2), 9–21.

Page, R. (1987). Teachers' perceptions of students: A link between classrooms, school cultures, and the social order. *Anthropology and Education Quarterly, 18,* 77–99.

Peske, H. G., Liu, E., Johnson, S. M., Kauffman, D., & Kardos, S. M. (2001). The next generation of teachers: Changing conceptions of a career in teaching. *Phi Delta Kappan, 83*(40), 304–311.

Porter, A. C., Youngs, P., & Odden, A. (2001). Advances in teacher assessments and their uses. In V. Richardson (Ed.), *Handbook of research on teaching,* 4th ed. Washington, DC: American Educational Research Association.

Schön, D. A. (1983). *The reflective practitioner.* New York: Basic Books.

Schön, D. A. (1987). *Educating the reflective practitioner: Toward a new design for teaching and learning in the professions.* San Francisco: Jossey-Bass.

Scriven, M. (1967). The methodology of evaluation. In R. Tyler, R. M. Gagne, & M. Scriven (Eds.), *Perspectives of curriculum evaluation.* Chicago: Rand McNally.

Shields, P. M., Humphrey, D. C., Wechsler, M. E., Riehl, L. M., Tiffany-Morales, J., Woodsworth, K., et al. (2001). *The status of the teaching profession 2001.* Santa Cruz, CA: The Center for the Future of Teaching and Learning.

Shulman, L. S. (1986). Those who understand: Knowledge growth in teaching. *Educational Researcher, 15*(2), 4–14.

Shulman, L. S. (1987). Knowledge and teaching: Foundations of the new reform. *Harvard Educational Review, 57*(1), 1–22.

Sleeter, C. E. (2001). Preparing teachers for culturally diverse schools: Research and the overwhelming presence of whiteness. *Journal of Teacher Education, 52*(2), 94–106.

Smylie, M. A., & Conyers, J. G. (1991). Changing conceptions of teaching influence the future of staff development. *Journal of Staff Development, 12*(1), 12–16.

Spencer, D. A. (2001). Teachers' work in historical context. In V. Richardson (Ed.), *Handbook of research on teaching,* 4th ed. Washington, DC: American Educational Research Association.

Stoddard, T. (1993). Who is prepared to teach in urban schools? *Education and Urban Society, 26*(1), 29–48.

Storms, B., & Lee, G. (2001). CFASST implementation and reflective practice: The interplay of structures and perceptions. *Issues in Teacher Education, 10*(2), 2–38.

Storms, B., Wing, J., Jinks, T., Banks, K., & Cavazos, P. (2000). *CFASST implementation 1999–2000: A formative evaluation report.* Unpublished report. Oakland, CA: Educational Testing Service.

Texas State Board for Educator Certification. (1998). *Final report on novice teacher induction support system.* Austin, TX: Author.

Thompson, C. L., & Zeuli, J. S. (1999). The frame and the tapestry. In L. Darling-Hammond & G. Sykes (Eds.), *Teaching as the learning profession: Handbook of policy and practice.* San Francisco: Jossey-Bass.

Treiman, J., Mahler, J., & Bartell, C. A. (2000, February). *Professional standards, portfolios, and reflective practice.* Paper presented at the annual meeting of the American Association of Colleges of Teacher Education, Chicago, IL.

Tushnet, N.C., Briggs, D., Elliot, J., Esch, C., Haviland, D., Humphrey, D.C., et al. (2002). *Final Report of the independent evaluation of the Beginning Teacher Support and Assessment Program (BTSA).* Los Alamitos, CA: WestEd.

U.S. Department of Education, Office of Postsecondary Education, Office of Policy, Planning, and Innovation. (2002). *Meeting the highly qualified teachers challenge: The secretary's annual report on teacher quality.* Washington, DC: Author.

Urban Teacher Collaborative. (2000). *The urban teacher challenge: Teacher demand and supply in the great city schools.* Belmont, MA: Recruiting New Teachers.

Valli, L. (1997). Listening to other voices: A description of teacher reflection in the United States. *Peabody Journal of Education, 72*(1), 67–88.

Veenman, S. (1984). Perceived problems of beginning teachers. *Review of Educational Research 54*(2), 143–178.

Watson, J. S., & Wilcox, S. (2000). Reading for understanding: Methods of reflecting on practice. *Reflective Practice, 1*(1), 57–67.

Weiner, L. (1999). *Urban Teaching: The Essentials.* New York: Teachers College Press.

Wing, J. Y., & Jinks, T. (2001). What skills, beliefs, and practices enable experienced teacher to promote reflective practice in novice teachers? *Issues in Teacher Education, 10*(2), 39–53.

Zachary, L. J. (2000). *The mentor's guide: Facilitating effective learning relationships.* San Francisco: Jossey-Bass.

Zeichner, K. (1993). *Educating teachers for cultural diversity.* East Lansing, MI: National Center for Research on Teacher Learning.

Zeichner, K. (1996). Teachers as reflective practitioners and the democratization of school reform. In I. Zeichner, S. Melcnick, & M. L. Gomez (Eds.), *Currents of reform in preservice teacher education.* New York: Teachers College Press.

Index

Accountability, 5
Achinstein, B., 105, 134, 135
Action research, 137
Administration:
  induction program support and, 48,
    49-50, 56, 97
  teacher-mentor matching task and,
    50, 59
  turnover within, 96-97
  urban schools and, 95
  See also Organizational context
Adult learning principles, 61-62,
  62 (exhibit)
Advancement opportunities, 10
Alternative career paths, 7-9, 37
  career stage variations and,
    40, 40 (exhibit)
  hard-to-staff positions and, 38
  induction needs in, 38-41, 52
  intern program and, 39, 110
  mentoring and, 87-90, 88-89 (exhibit)
  preparation/induction, merging
    of, 109-111
  preparation programs, 37-38, 90
  professional development requirements
    and, 62-63
  quality/impact of, 37
  student-teaching experience and, 38
  teacher shortages and, 37, 38
Assessment, 8, 45
  mentor responsibility and, 65
  See also Teacher assessment
Ayers, W., 108

Ball, D. L., 138
Baron, W., 60
Barrett, A., 105, 134, 135
Bartell, C. A., 89, 100
Beginning teachers, 1

alternate career paths and, 7-9, 37-41
career choice, motivation and, 9-11
case example, 1-3
challenges of, 3-4, 12-14
collaborative model and, 11-12
conditional approach of, 10-11
contributing orientation and, 11
exploring orientation and, 11
multicultural/diverse teaching
  contexts and, 12-14
national standards for, 121-123,
  122 (exhibit)
needs of, 16-18, 17 (exhibit)
preparation needs, 6-7, 18-19
preparation-practice bridge and, 33-34
professional development opportunities
  and, 61-63, 62-64 (exhibits)
psychological stages of, 34-35,
  35 (exhibit)
quality of, 5
responsibilities, staging of, 3
school context and, 35-36
teacher shortage and, 4-5
See also Effective induction programs;
  Induction programs; Mentoring;
  Teacher development
Beginning Teacher Support and
  Assessment (BTSA) program, xiii,
  45-46, 47 (exhibit)
  assessment system, 154-159,
    155-156 (exhibit)
  evaluation of, 109-110
  standards-based teaching and, 123-124,
    125-146 (exhibit)
Berliner, D. C., 26, 27, 28, 29
Best practices, 81, 83
  See also Mentoring
Briggs, D., 56, 149, 151, 159
Bryk, A. S., 138

Burden, P. W., 29
Burnout, 34, 35

California Commission on Teacher
    Credentialing, 83, 86, 124, 154, 167
California Formative Assessment
    and Support System for
    Teachers (CFASST), 47, 157-159,
    158-159 (exhibit)
California induction program. *See*
    Beginning Teacher Support and
    Assessment (BTSA) program
California New Teacher Project (CNTP),
    123, 156
California Standards for Induction
    Programs, 77
California Standards of the Teaching
    Profession (CSTP), 47, 83, 121, 124,
    125-126 (exhibit)
    Learning to Teach System, 170-172,
        171 (exhibit)
    reflective practice and, 130-131,
        130 (exhibit)
    teacher assessment and, 154,
        155-156 (exhibit)
    See also Interstate New Teacher
        Assessment and Support
        Consortium (INTASC)
Career paths, 7-9
Career stages, 24-26, 26 (exhibit)
    traditional vs. alternate-path teachers,
        40, 40 (exhibit)
    See also Beginning teachers
Carnegie Forum on Education and the
    Economy, 148
Certification. *See* Credentialing process
Christiansen, J., 25, 26, 29, 30
Cohen, D. K., 138
Collaborative environment, 11-12
    induction service partnerships and,
        48-49, 56
    preparation/induction, merging of,
        110-111
    reflective practice and, 138-139
    university linkages and, 50-52
Collective bargaining agreements, 55-56
Collegial relationships, 57, 72, 97, 137
Collins, K., 154
Compensation. *See* Monetary
    compensation
Context. *See* Organizational context;
    School context
Continuing education, 22-23
Continuous improvement, 46

Contributing orientation, 11
Credentialing process, xvi, 4
    alternate career paths and, 7-9, 37, 38
    Federal policy and, 172-173
    induction assessment and, 146
    lifetime credentials, 22
    teacher quality and, 5
Crosby, E. A., 100
Cultural competency, 106-107, 107 (exhibit)
Cultural context, 12, 94-95
    culturally sensitive curriculum and,
        105, 106
    See also Diversity; Urban schools
Curriculum standards, 8
    culturally responsive curriculum and,
        105, 106
    reflective practice and, 118
    urban schools and, 97

Daresh, J. D., 79
Darling-Hammond, L., 39, 120, 144
Development. *See* Professional
    development; Teacher development
Dewey, J., 117
Disillusionment, 34, 35, 98
Diversity:
    student populations and, 4, 104, 106
    teaching contexts and, 12-13
    urban schools and, 99-100, 101
Doolittle, F., 93

Educational Testing Service, 157
Effective induction programs, 43-44, 66, 68
    collaborative partnerships and, 48-49, 56
    contextual factors, attention to, 53-58
    coordinated efforts and, 49
    feedback and, 65
    leadership in, 47-48
    mentoring role/responsibilities and,
        58-59, 64-65
    organization of, 44-45
    professional development opportunities
        and, 61-63, 62-64 (exhibits)
    program evaluation and, 65-66,
        67 (exhibit)
    purposes of, 45-46, 47 (exhibit)
    site administrator support and, 49-50
    time-structuring in, 59-61
    university linkages and, 49, 50-52
    See also Mentoring
Elliot, J., 56, 149, 151, 159
Elmore, R. F., 119
English as a second language (ESL),
    94-95, 99

Erikson, E., 24
Esch, C., 56, 149, 151, 159
Expectations, 97, 105, 124
Expertise development, 26-29, 27 (exhibit)
Exploring orientation, 11

Feedback, 45, 65
Feiman-Nemser, S., 25, 29, 56, 75, 115, 134
Fendler, L., 135
Fessler, R., 25, 26, 29, 30
Fideler, E. F., 101, 104
Floden, R. E., 56
Ford, P., 108
Formative assessments, 148-149, 155-156
    (exhibit), 156-159, 158-159 (exhibit)
Fuller, F. F., 24, 25, 29
Full inclusion, 14
Funding streams:
    general vs. special education, 14
    induction programs and, 48, 172
    mentor compensation and, 81
    mentoring support and, 60, 80
    See also Resource allocation

Gless, J., 60
Gold, Y., 34
Government policy, 5
    induction plans, 15, 16, 44
    urban schools and, 95
    See also Induction policies

Haberman, M., 100, 108
Haselkorn, D., 101, 104
Haviland, D., 56, 149, 151, 159
Hawley, W. D., 64
Herlihy, C., 93
Hidalgo, F., 108
High expectations, 97, 105
Holton, E. F., 62
Huberman, M., 49
Huling, L., 73, 76, 78
Humphrey, D. C., 56, 149, 151, 159

Individualized Induction Plan (IIP),
    47, 83, 84 (exhibit), 156
Induction policies, 165, 176
    development of, California, 170-172,
        171 (exhibit)
    Federal role in, 172-173
    funding and, 172
    future policy, 175
    implementation challenges, 174-175
    local policies, 168, 169 (exhibit)
    practice applications of, 173-175

state policy framework, 168, 170
teacher/student success and, 167, 174-175
vision for, 165-167
Induction programs, xiv, xvi, 5-6
    alternate-path teachers and, 37-41
    beginning teachers, needs of, 16-18,
        17 (exhibit)
    benefits of, 16
    career commitment goal of, 11, 34
    collaborative model and, 11-12
    discovery and, 32-33
    future of, 175
    mandatory requirement of, 15-16
    preparation levels and, 6-7
    reflective practice and, 132-133
    stage theory application and, 29-30,
        29 (exhibit)
    success-orientation of, 8-9
    survival and, 32
    teacher development and, 23, 29-30,
        29 (exhibit), 32-33
    teacher motivation and, 14-15
    teaching contexts and, 14
    urban school settings and, 101-104,
        103 (exhibit)
    See also Effective induction programs;
        Mentoring
Ingersoll, R. M., 101
Instructional resources, 13, 98, 99
Intern programs, 39, 110
Interstate New Teacher Assessment and
    Support Consortium (INTASC), 16,
    121-123, 122 (exhibit), 128
    accreditation standards and, 173
    disposition and, 129, 129 (exhibit)
    knowledge requirements, 128
    professional practices/responsibilities
        and, 129-130
    reflective practice and, 129
    teacher assessment, 153-154

Jinks, T., 129, 148
Johnson, S. M., 10
Joyce, B. R., 64

Katz, L., 25, 29
Kemmis, S., 137
Klein, S. P., 144
Knowles, M. S., 62
Kruse, S. D., 138

Learning to Teach System, 170-172,
    171 (exhibit)
Lee, G., 116

Lifelong learning, 5, 23, 118
Lindsey, R. B., 106, 107
Little, J. W., 36, 72, 138
Long-term commitment, 11
Los Angeles Unified School District, 88, 88-89 (exhibit)
Louis, K. S., 138

Mager, G. M., 133
McCormick, R. S., 117, 157
McTaggart, R., 137
Mentoring, xiv, 15, 38, 71, 90-91
    alternate-path teachers and, 87-90, 88-89 (exhibit)
    benefits of, 73-75
    best practices and, 81, 83
    boundary-setting and, 78
    challenges in, 86-87
    compensation for, 81
    concept of, 72-73
    follow-up/feedback and, 64-65
    individualized plan development, 83, 84 (exhibit), 86
    induction programs and, 71-72
    intensity levels of, 83, 85 (exhibit), 86
    mentor selection, 75-79, 77 (exhibit), 79 (exhibit), 86
    mentor training, 77-79, 78 (exhibit)
    reflective mentoring, 131-132, 133
    role/responsibilities in, 50, 59
    site administrator support and, 49-50
    structured programming and, 59-61, 74-75
    teacher-mentor matching, 79-80, 86-87
    teacher observation and, 60-61, 80-81, 82 (exhibit)
    time-structuring and, 59-61, 80-81, 87
    university supervision and, 52
    urban school settings and, 95, 107-109
    vision in, 75
Moir, E., 35, 60
Monetary compensation, 10, 81
Moss, P. A., 154
Motivation, 9-11
    induction programs and, 14-15
    urban school settings and, 97

National Association of State Directors of Teacher Education and Certification, 147
National Board for Professional Teaching Standards, 144, 148, 154
National Commission on Professional Development and Support of Novice Teachers, 76

National Commission on Teaching and America's Future, 4, 119
National Council on Accreditation for Teacher Education (NCATE), 173
New teachers. See Beginning teachers
No Child Left Behind Act, 173
Nuri Robins, K., 106, 107

Observation of teaching, 60-61, 80-81, 82 (exhibit), 137, 151
Odden, A., 144, 160
Odell, S. J., 73, 76, 78
Organizational context, 31, 36
    induction program leadership and, 47-48
    See also School context; Urban schools

Page, R., 56
Parental involvement, 57-58
Partnerships, 49
    parental involvement, 57-58
    university linkages, 50-52
Peer Assistance and Review (PAR) programs, 124
Performance-based assessment, 145, 148, 152, 160
Policy. See Government policy; Induction policies
Porter, A. C., 144, 160
Portfolio assessment, 150, 153-154
Preparation programs, 3
    components of, 6-7
    diverse teaching contexts and, 12-14
    lifelong learning and, 5, 23
    practice applications and, 33-34
    preparation/induction merging, 109-111
    preservice programs, 7
    teacher shortages and, 4
    See also Alternative career paths
Preservice programs, 7, 52
Problem-based learning, 137-138
Professional artistry, 117-118
Professional development:
    adult learning principles, 61-62, 62 (exhibit)
    beginning teachers and, 61-64
    career stages and, 25-26
    cultural competency and, 106-107, 107 (exhibit)
    effectiveness elements, 64 (exhibit)
    induction program support and, 48
    mentor training, 77-79, 78 (exhibit)
    orientation, group approach, 62, 63 (exhibit)
    rural areas and, 13-14
    See also Teacher development

Professionalization movement, 23
Program evaluation, 45
    induction programs and, 65-66,
        67 (exhibit)
    See also Teacher assessment
Psychological stages, 34-35, 35 (exhibit)

Recruitment efforts, 4
    motivated individuals, identification of,
        9-10, 11
    rural isolation and, 13-14
    urban settings and, 99
Reflective practice, 116-118, 124, 140
    collaborative professional community
        and, 138-139
    induction phase and, 132-133, 135-136
    mentoring and, 131-132
    national standards and, 128-130,
        129 (exhibit)
    problems with, 134-135
    state standards and, 130-131, 130 (exhibit)
    teacher assessments and, 160-161
    tools for, 136-138
Reform. See School reform
Resource allocation, 55
    mentoring practices and, 60
    See also Funding streams
Retention of personnel, 3, 4
    disillusionment/burnout and, 34
    intrinsic rewards and, 10
    long-term career commitment, 11
    special education and, 14
    teaching contexts, challenges
        of, 12-14
    urban school context and, 95-97, 99
    See also Effective induction programs;
        Induction programs; Mentoring
Rural settings, 13-14

Schön, D. A., 117
School context, 35-36, 53, 58
    class size, 54
    collegial relationships and, 57
    district policies and, 55-56
    parental involvement and, 57-58
    physical plant deterioration, 56-57
    resource availability, 55
    school climate, 56-57
    school type, 53-54
    student characteristics, 55-56
    teacher workload, 54-55
    See also Urban schools
School reform:
    implementation, teacher preparation
        and, 22-23

instructional coherence and, 98
    leadership in, 95
    urban public schools and, 93-94
School-university linkages, 50-52
Schutz, A. M., 154
Scriven, M., 148
Showers, B., 64
Sleeter, C. E., 12
Snipes, J., 93
Social services, 4
Special education, 14
Staff development. See Professional
    development; Teacher development
Stage theory, 24-26, 26 (exhibit)
    induction phase and, 29-30, 29 (exhibit)
    psychological stages and, 34-35,
        35 (exhibit)
Standardized testing, 5
Standards-based teaching, 115, 139-140
    compliance effecting vs. capacity
        enhancing focus of, 118-119
    design/interpretation of, 120
    induction programs and, 115-116,
        120-121
    national standards, new teachers and,
        121-123, 122 (exhibit), 128-130,
        129 (exhibit)
    peer review programs, 124
    professional development/practice and,
        124, 127
    reflective mentoring, 131-132
    state standards, California, 123-124,
        125-126 (exhibit), 130-131,
        130 (exhibit)
    student standards and, 127-128
    See also Reflective practice; Teacher
        assessment
Standards movement, 5, 119
Standards of Quality and Effectiveness
    for Teacher Induction
    Programs, 154
Stoddard, T., 105
Stroms, B., 116
Student success, xii, xvi
    induction programs and, 46, 47
    standardized testing, 5
    standards of achievement and, 127-128
    student mobility patterns and, 98
    teaching quality and, 5
    urban schools and, 94-95
    workforce preparation focus, 4-5
Student-teaching, 3, 7
    alternative path careers and, 38
    university supervision of, 52
Summative assessments, 148-149

Support providers, 3
  experienced teachers, 58-59
  site-administrators, 48, 49-50
  university linkages, 51-52
Survival, xvi, 3, 15, 32, 88
Swanson, R. A., 62

Teacher assessment, 143, 161-162
  content-specific/portfolio-based
    assessment, 153-154
  evaluation and, 145
  formative assessment systems, 155-156
    (exhibit), 156-159, 158-159 (exhibit)
  formative vs. summative assessments,
    148-149
  induction assessments, 146-147
  local development of, 159-160
  methods of, 149-152
  ongoing performance evaluations,
    147-148
  performance-based assessment, 145
  purposes of, 144-145
  reflective practice and, 160-161
  standards-driven assessment,
    143-145
  state assessment system, 154-159,
    155-156 (exhibit), 158-159 (exhibit)
  student learning and, 145
Teacher development, xii, xvi, 21, 41-42
  alternative-path teachers and, 37-41
  continuing education and, 22-23
  cultural competency and, 106-107,
    107 (exhibit)
  disillusionment/burnout and, 34, 35, 98
  expertise, developmental stages in,
    26-29, 27 (exhibit)
  induction phase and, 29-30, 29
    (exhibit), 32-33
  organizational factors in, 31
  personal factors in, 30-31
  preparation-practice bridge, 33-34
  preparation programs and, 21-22
  professionalization of teaching and, 23
  psychological stages, novice teachers
    and, 34-35, 35 (exhibit)
  reform implementation and, 22-23
  responsibilities, staging of, 3
  school context and, 35-36
  stage theory of development and, 24-26,
    26 (exhibit), 29-30
  See also Beginning teachers; Effective
    induction programs; Induction
    programs; Professional
    development

Teacher shortage, 4-5
  alternative career paths and, 37, 38
  special education field, 14
Technology, 13, 174
Terrell, R. D., 106, 107
Thompson, C. L., 137
Tushnet, N. C., 56, 149, 151, 159

University partnerships, 49, 50-52, 104,
  111, 124
Urban schools, 3, 12-13, 38, 57, 111-112
  academic achievement levels
    and, 94-95
  administrative turnover rates
    and, 96-97
  characteristics of, 94
  cultural competency and, 106-107,
    107 (exhibit)
  curriculum, cultural sensitivity of,
    105, 106
  diversity issues in, 104-106
  facility/neighborhood concerns,
    98-99
  induction programs and, 93-94,
    101-104, 103 (exhibit)
  instructional resources and, 99
  low expectations/curricular deficits
    and, 97
  mentoring programs in, 107-109
  political context of, 95
  reform, instructional coherence
    and, 98
  student mobility patterns and, 98
  teacher choice of, 100-101
  teacher preparation/induction, merging
    of, 109-111
  teacher-student matching in, 99-100
  teacher turnover/inexperience and,
    95-96, 100, 102

Valli, L., 64, 131
Veenman, S., 25
Vision, 75

Wages. See Monetary compensation
Wing, J. Y., 129, 148
Wise, A. E., 144
Workforce preparation, 4-5

Youngs, P., 144, 160

Zachary, L. J., 79
Zeichner, K., 105
Zeuli, J. S., 137